The Lord of SPIRITS

An Orthodox Christian Framework for the Unseen World and Spiritual Warfare

ANDREW STEPHEN DAMICK

ANCIENT FAITH PUBLISHING
CHESTERTON, INDIANA

The Lord of Spirits: An Orthodox Christian Framework for the Unseen World and Spiritual Warfare

Published by:
Ancient Faith Publishing
A Division of Ancient Faith Ministries
1050 Broadway, Suite 6
Chesterton, IN 46304

ISBN: 978-1-955890-53-3

Library of Congress Control Number: 2023940705

Illustration and cover design by Samuel Heble.

For Raphael Joseph Cædmon,
the Dragon Slayer

Table of Contents

Now as [Heliodorus] was there present himself with his guard about the treasury, the Lord of Spirits, and the Prince of all power, caused a great apparition, so that all that presumed to come in with him were astonished at the power of God, and fainted, and were sore afraid.

—2 Maccabees 3:24 (KJV)

He will be a staff for the righteous with which for them to stand and not to fall. And he will be the light of the nations and the hope of those whose hearts are troubled. All who dwell on the earth will fall down and worship him, and they will praise and bless and celebrate with song the Lord of Spirits.

—1 Enoch 48:4–5[1]

1 From an unpublished translation by Fr. Stephen De Young.

Foreword

Really, there's no such thing as "cradle Orthodox." A handful of saints in the history of the world have been born saints, having a fully formed relationship with God from the womb, e.g. the prophet Jeremiah, the Theotokos, and St. John, the Forerunner. The rest of us must all convert. The rest of us pursue a life of repentance. The rest of us, regardless of whether we grew up surrounded by Holy Tradition or whether we discovered the Christian way of life later in our lives, have to consciously embrace it and work to make it our own.

This has always been the case. The first generation of Israelites was, in modern terms, an ethnically diverse group. They stood at the base of Mt. Sinai on the first Pentecost and received the covenant of the Torah from God. There they converted and became Israelites. Every subsequent generation likewise needed to become sons of the covenant. The greater mass of the original tribes of Israel, historically, ultimately ceased to be Israelites and abandoned their heritage. Throughout the Old Testament, members of nations, tribes, and clans outside of Israel were grafted in and became Israelites; they converted in an obvious, visible way. But the sons and daughters of pious parents converted in a way no less real, by receiving the Tradition handed on to them and making its way of life their own.

On the second Pentecost, likewise, thousands of Jewish people gathered from around the Roman world in Jerusalem made Christ and the fulfillment and transformation He brought to their Jewish way of life their own. The Tradition these first Christians passed down to their children and their children's children included the teaching of the apostles about the Lord Jesus Christ. These succeeding generations grew up within Christian worshiping communities. They followed the Christian way of life within their families. The day came for each one, however, when they needed to make that Tradition and way of life their own in preparation for passing it on to the generation that came after. The day came when each of them had to convert.

In every generation of Christian history, people from outside the Tradition have also entered Christian communities and made the Christian Faith and way of life their own. At the same time, in every generation, facing hardships, disillusionment, and persecution, some who had previously been a part of Christian communities forsook the Tradition that had been handed on to them, and they departed. Throughout all these challenges, shifts, and changes to society—internal and external threats—the Church has endured and has preserved Holy Tradition for each new generation of Christians.

The task of this generation of Orthodox Christians, as for all the others, is to make the depth and riches of Tradition our own. This is a collective work that the whole Church of this generation works toward together. Each member of the Body of Christ has some element of this work to which they are able to contribute. Some are gifted to explore and articulate the teaching of the Church Fathers from various past generations. Some are able to contextualize and teach the rich traditions of music and iconography we have inherited. Others gain and describe a deep understanding of our Liturgy and its celebration.

From its beginning, *The Lord of Spirits* podcast has aimed to make a contribution to this generation's appropriation of the Orthodox Faith. The podcast has focused on exploring and communicating the Church's understanding of the Holy Scriptures and her self-understanding of her cultural and social history in the world. To be an Orthodox Christian requires not only being able to repeat certain formulae or know the right answers to certain questions regarding doctrine and history. It is certainly more than just being a member of the right team. We must come to understand our Holy Tradition, to become vessels for it, to live it out in our own lives, and most importantly, to be prepared to pass it on to the next generation of Christians to likewise make it their own. As a distillation, this book is another step toward this end.

Christ has promised that every scribe trained for the Kingdom of heaven will be like the master of a house who is able to bring treasures both new and old out of his treasury (Matt. 13:52). The new treasures are not new in the sense of never before existing, nor in the sense of changing or contradicting the old. These are, within Christ's own statement, treasures that already exist and have been safeguarded in the treasury. They are new in the sense that St. John's commandment is new (1 John 2:7–8). Holy Tradition is always the same, unchanging, but at the same time always new and transformative to each new generation that converts to become followers of Christ.

—V. Rev. Dr. Stephen De Young

Preface

IN THE FALL OF 2020, the Ancient Faith Radio (AFR) podcast *The Lord of Spirits* launched, featuring conversations between biblical scholar Fr. Stephen De Young and me about the Bible and other ancient texts within the context of the Orthodox Christian Tradition. The focus is mainly on the unseen spiritual world of angels, demons, and saints—realities that most Christians believe in but that don't get much coverage in modern sermons and other Christian discussion.

When we originally pitched the idea to AFR leadership, they responded that the topic seemed a little "niche." Would anyone be interested? We honestly weren't sure ourselves. Despite the skepticism, though, the podcast came together, and its first episode aired live on September 10, 2020, just as so much despair was setting in due to the isolation caused by the response to the coronavirus pandemic. Since then, listenership has grown to probably the largest of any Orthodox podcast in the English language. The scale of the response truly surprised all of us.

I mention this because it revealed to us that at this moment there is an enormous hunger for content related to the spiritual world as the Orthodox Church has always understood it. Understanding our present moment in history in its full complexity is a task best left to future thinkers, but one thing about it is clear: a growing number of people have a sense that the unseen spiritual world—especially in terms of demonic activity—is intruding upon the world that we do see. With the pandemic isolation, an already disenchanted world was losing the last enchantment most people had—simply being with one another. Yet despite this disenchantment, we cannot deny the demonic.

I believe this is why the podcast has had such a sudden and surprisingly strong positive response. The podcast's combination of mainstream biblical scholarship, mythological studies, patristic writings, and Orthodox liturgical tradition communicates that the Christian life happens within a coherent world that is whole, humane, and holy, comprising both the seen and unseen in a single whole.

In a true sense, the podcast communicates nothing new—even the biblical scholarship Fr. Stephen researches and presents most often simply reveals what the early Church and subsequent Orthodox Tradition have known and even taken for granted. As we like to say (just a little sarcastically), it turns out that the Bible is Orthodox. And it also turns out that we're not making this stuff up.

To give just one example, you can sometimes hear among Orthodox immigrants to the West what is sometimes dismissed as an "old wives' tale"—that the saints take the place of the fallen angels in the heavenly hosts. I have heard this explained away as "folk theology." Yet how many times do we hear in liturgical hymns to the saints that they are now rejoicing with the angels? In a resurrectional theotokion in tone 4 for Saturday Great Vespers, we sing that Christ goes to find the lost sheep to "add it through His will to the heavenly hosts." And Christ Himself says in Luke 20:36 that Christians become "equal to angels." Part of what we do on the podcast is show that all these elements we already have as Orthodox Christians are in fact connected and convey something that the wise once knew and "old wives" sometimes repeat.

By the time this book is published, the podcast *The Lord of Spirits* will be about three years old, covering close to 200 hours of material. This book, despite having the same title, is not a recap of all that information. That would make for an impossibly large tome.

This book is also not an overview of *all* the key concepts we discuss on the podcast. Again, that is because that would still be a huge book, but it is also because I don't feel myself qualified to delve into every one of the subjects we've covered on the show. I am still a learner myself (which is basically my usual role in the show).

So what is this book? It is the material from the podcast that I speak about myself most often in my preaching and teaching, in public lectures and conversations. It is also new material you won't have heard on the podcast, based on my own research and on the application of my conversations with Fr. Stephen, particularly the portions focused on mythology, literature, and evangelism.

All that said, if you have never listened to *The Lord of Spirits* podcast, don't worry. This book is designed to stand on its own. And if you have listened to every episode of the podcast, don't worry, because you will encounter new material here. I also believe that even material you already know will be helpfully summarized here in a way you can refer back to when needed.

Apart from the podcast, this book is in a sense a sequel to my little book *Arise, O God: The Gospel of Christ's Defeat of Demons, Sin, and Death* (Ancient Faith Publishing, 2021), though again, if you haven't read it, this book still stands on its own. That book describes the gospel.

In this book, I focus on giving a framework for beginning to understand the unseen side of the world in which Christ's rescue of humankind from demons and their influence happens, to try as much as possible to recover something of ancient people's understanding when they first heard the Scriptures. Further, I strive to show how the defeat of the demons and our rescue from them work out in terms of spiritual warfare. Most importantly, I hope that the reader will gain a better sense of how to be faithful to Christ within this context.

In addition to this book, I commend to the reader Fr. Stephen's related texts from Ancient Faith Publishing: *The Religion of the*

Apostles (a single-volume Orthodox biblical theology), *The Whole Counsel of God* (an examination of the Scriptures as a text), and *Apocrypha* (an overview of the Second Temple literature that forms the basis of much of the theology in *The Religion of the Apostles*). Readers of *The Religion of the Apostles* will recognize some of the same themes in parts of this present book, though I often structure them differently and treat them from other angles.

For this book I am of course in debt to Fr. Stephen for his writings and the many conversations I have had with him. Thanks also go to the Rev. Dr. Joseph Lucas, who read through this manuscript and gave me comments especially on my use of the Church Fathers. I am also in debt to the many listeners of *The Lord of Spirits* podcast, with all your enthusiasm, in-jokes, unofficial T-shirts, and bat costumes. May God grant every one of you many years.

Unless otherwise noted, names of Old Testament books and the numbering of the Psalms in this book are according to the Hebrew Old Testament rather than the Greek because that is familiar to most English speakers and is in their Bibles. To "convert" the naming or numbering (especially for the Psalms) to what is read aloud in Orthodox churches, consult the tables in the *Orthodox Study Bible* or other comparative resources. The content, in any event, is essentially the same in most respects.

Scriptural quotations are from the English Standard Version (ESV) of the Bible except where otherwise noted. I may also refer to variations found in the Greek Old Testament (sometimes the *Septuagint,* though that refers properly only to the first five books) (LXX) or the Dead Sea Scrolls (DSS).

—Archpriest Andrew Stephen Damick
Emmaus, Pennsylvania
Great and Holy Pascha 2023

INTRODUCTION

The Christian and the Dragon

In that day the Lord *with his hard and great and strong sword will punish Leviathan the fleeing serpent, Leviathan the twisting serpent, and he will slay the dragon that is in the sea.*

—Isaiah 27:1

The Cross is the trophy of victory against the demons, the sword against sin, the blade wherewith Christ smote the serpent.

—St. John Chrysostom[1]

There are dragons in the Christian tradition. It should be obvious that Christians should take them seriously, since we find these great wyrms in the Scriptures, not to mention in traditional liturgical texts, the writings of the Church Fathers, and iconography.

1 Saint John Chrysostom, "Homily On the Cemetery and the Cross (Excerpts)," in *Orthodox Christianity Then and Now,* May 3, 2011, www.johnsanidopoulos.com/2011/05/st-john-chrysostoms-homily-on-cemetery.html.

Suddenly the peaceful, mundane world of Sunday School flannelgraph Bible stories gets a lot scarier.

It gets worse, though. Alongside these biblical dragons such as Leviathan and the devil, we find other monsters such as Behemoth, the great demon of tyranny, and Lilith, the night demon of sterility. And if we look at the pagan religious world the prophets and apostles knew, we also find werewolves, vampires, and zombies. But as the Scriptures tell us, we also are surrounded by "so great a cloud of witnesses" (Heb. 12:1)—the angels and saints. While this unseen world indeed teems with monsters, the Archangel Michael turns his flaming sword to the dragon, and he casts the great serpent out from the presence of God and His divine council. Saint George also turns his spear against the beast, and he slays it and turns it back from the faithful.

Although such images and their accompanying stories are plentiful in the traditional texts and iconography of Christianity, for most in the twenty-first century who approach them, Christian or not, they have become opaque: fantastical mythology that has no place except in that part of the imagination that is useful for moral formation or, more often, entertainment. Dragons have no part in the waking life of the serious person, or even the serious Christian, who can explain them as poetic imagery meant to convey some inner truth that nonetheless has no actual presence in the "real" world.

To the modern mind, dragons and demons are just the "inner demons" of psychology. And angels are often reducible to the "better angels of our nature," that is, to our better human impulses and virtues—again, talk of spirits is really about psychology. Or in some cases, people may use these terms to refer to social phenomena, the psychology of communities in their function and dysfunction. But to the ancient mind of millennia ago, even up to the pre-modern mind of just centuries ago, these are real beings with personal presence who inhabit our world and affect us. The people who first heard the

Scriptures and the Christians who creatively reflected on them in the centuries that followed believed in dragons.

As one looks at the mythic stories of Scripture and elsewhere in Christian tradition, one looks in vain for some moment that an apostle, prophet, saint, or even an iconographer or hymnographer pulls back the curtain to reveal that all this is simply a metaphor. At no point do they say, "We all know that dragons and werewolves don't actually exist, so please read these as colorful metaphors." Instead, we get a coherent, consistently depicted world in which spiritual beings, including monsters, were simply part of the world. They do not make arguments for the existence of these spiritual beings, because everyone in that world knew they existed. A close look at the way these stories are expressed also reveals that they do not speak of dragons in terms of having heard a story from someone else but rather in terms of real experience. The dragons of the Bible and of other stories from the ancient world were dragons that real people met, and they later went on to tell the tale.

Christians who try to take these stories seriously may acknowledge them to be true on some level—after all, these creatures are everywhere in their Tradition. But most of the time, they do not put these creatures into the center of their Christian life, despite their ubiquity in the Tradition. The Christian life is thus a journey of the person toward and with Christ, with angels as occasional helpers and demons as enemies who try to hinder the quest. The Hero's Journey is the model for the Christian, whose story is about him or herself. Spirits are marginal characters whose presence or absence does not fundamentally alter the plot.

To many Christians, these spirits of course exist, but Christianity is not about encountering them and relating to them. For most, the divine consists of the Father, Son, and Holy Spirit—and pretty much no one else. The divine council that the Scriptures depict is an obscure topic that might be related to heaven somehow, yet it doesn't penetrate into the daily life of the Christian, who is trying to get his or her soul saved. This kind of Christianity might have saints on the calendar but not in the living room.

That image of what it means to be Christian is not congruent with the pre-modern understanding, however, in which the Christian life is about being raised up to become part of the divine council, to be "sons of God," "equal to angels" (Luke 20:36). And because this individualistic version of Christianity does not have a robust understanding of the spiritual realm that is populated with a lot more beings than just the soul and God, the Christian who believes in this way may at some point find that this mythic language is scandalous in his or her tradition. He or she may also fall prey to criticisms of Christianity that ridicule a mythic imagery of faith that he or she is unready to defend.

The modern age is sometimes said to be an age of unbelief, and certainly, there is a clear waxing of atheism as well as disaffiliation with religious bodies. The demonstrable belief in the unseen during the whole pre-modern period, universally throughout the world, is explained as devotion to the "god(s) of the gaps," gaps that scientific knowledge now fills. Ancient people believed in dragons because they had no other explanation for the roiling of the sea or for crocodiles. They believed in gods because they saw lightning or felt earthquakes and assumed these must be the anger of unseen deities. They believed in creation myths because they could not fathom a big bang or biological evolution. They had never actually seen any gods or spoken with them, yet they still told stories about them. At some point in the distant past, someone told a lie or just dreamed up these gods. Then these stories got repeated over millennia, with no one really questioning if they were true, despite actual evidence never showing up. Pre-modern people apparently did not care about evidence.

But at some point people began to care about evidence and started questioning whether these stories of the gods were true. The scientific exploration of the world began, and people found that electric charges caused lightning, weather patterns caused storms in the sea, and biology provided the explanation for the variety of life. Modern people are therefore more educated with scientific discoveries of naturalistic, material causes, so they no longer feel the need for myths. That is how the modern world depicts religion in the ancient one and explains why we longer need it. We have simply outgrown it because we have more credible explanations for things.

Yet the history of scientific exploration and discovery did not begin just a few centuries ago. Most of scientific history happened in ages fully immersed in belief in an unseen world of spirits. The "god(s) of the gaps" narrative cannot explain how scientific knowledge of natural causes throughout most of history (and even now) existed alongside belief in and ritual participation with spiritual beings.

Further, that depiction of ancient religion is not how ancient people themselves talked about their experience of the world. They did not tell a series of tales trying to explain natural phenomena. They did not offer collections of stories and rituals based on suppositions. Rather, what one consistently sees is ancient people saying that they had real encounters with spiritual beings who actually spoke to them in a language they could understand. They not only told stories but also conducted rituals that put them into direct contact with their gods.

Despite the loss of religious membership, opinion polls consistently show that spiritual beliefs of various kinds are not really waning to any appreciable degree. Belief in an unseen world that exists and is important to us has survived the challenges of the past few centuries. Despite the public discourse of a modern world that assumes a flat materialism, those who inhabit it nevertheless remain haunted by angels, demons, and saints. In terms of what we take seriously as "real life," these spirits are perhaps just on the edge of our consciousness. But in our cultural output, they are positively thronging on every side. The stories we tell of wizards, elves, dwarves, fairies, orcs, trolls, superheroes, and space aliens are all attempts to come to terms with this haunting we feel, the sense that there is something just beyond our physical sight.

From a traditional Christian point of view, or even one looking from historical paganism, these stories often get stuff profoundly wrong (a Norse pagan would find Marvel's Thor movies almost incomprehensible), but for some reason, we keep trying. We keep trying to understand the sense we have that the visible is accompanied by the invisible, that the latter is not some other world of pure imagination but actually is present within our own world.

The Christian tradition has a coherent, consistent account of what that unseen world is about and how we should properly relate to it. Christians and those learning about Christianity therefore have an interest in appropriating that account for themselves. What is more, this appropriation is indeed possible by taking a close look at that Tradition and by engaging in its living community. We do not have to look at all the dragons in the Bible and feel embarrassed by them or explain them away as metaphorical stories. To be sure, as modern people we cannot flip a switch and begin perceiving the world and thinking like pre-modern people. Nor can reading a book accomplish this purpose. But we can provide a framework for understanding what to us seem like the bizarre and astounding elements of Christian tradition, elements that were, so to speak, simply part of the air ancient people breathed. And if we embrace that framework and, more importantly, become faithful to the life into which it is embedded, then a whole new world opens up in front of us.

People who have been Christian their whole lives may experience having their minds blown by what has been in front of us all this time.

For those who are just learning about Christianity, it may be the first time they hear that the demons they already know and struggle with are already well-known by the Church and, even more, that the Church's Christ has already defeated them.

Life in Christ is thus not a journey that happens with angels and demons on the periphery. Rather, it means that He rescues us from slavery to demonic forces. Life in Christ means joining Him and His angels as He defeats His demonic enemies. The purpose of this book is to begin to provide this framework so that we not only have a better understanding of the unseen world but that we live well within it, integrating what we have learned to become more faithful to Christ, who is the Lord of Spirits.

CHAPTER 1

The Lord of Hosts: God and the Gods

Who is like you, O [Yahweh],[1] *among the gods? Who is like you, majestic in holiness, awesome in glorious deeds, doing wonders?*

—Exodus 15:11

They are no gods, who do not what is right.

—Euripides[2]

---

1 *Yahweh* is the name in Hebrew for God used throughout the Old Testament, coming from the "to be" verb. It is often translated in Bibles as "the Lord" and in Orthodox liturgical texts (based on the Greek translation of the Old Testament) as "the Existing One" or "the One who is." The form *Yahweh* has a causative sense, i.e., "the One who causes things to be," that is, the Creator. The first-person form *Ahyeh* ("I am") is how God introduces Himself to Moses (Ex. 3:14). Some Christians, following later rabbinical Jewish tradition, will not write or pronounce *Yahweh*, but Scriptures and early Christian tradition do not prohibit it.

2 Euripides, *Bellerophon*, as cited by St. Justin Martyr in *On the Sole Government of God*, ch. 5, in *Ante-Nicene Fathers*, trans. and ed. Alexander Roberts, James Donaldson, and A. Cleveland Coxe, vol. 1 (Peabody, MA: Hendrickson Publishers, 1999), 292.

An atheist internet pop-apologetic against Christianity goes like this: "I contend we are both atheists, I just believe in one fewer god than you do. When you understand why you dismiss all the other possible gods, you will understand why I dismiss yours." This statement first appeared in a 1990s debate on Usenet, an early social media network, between atheist Stephen F. Roberts and religious believers on the alt.atheism newsgroup.[3] The apologetic means that, since most people who believe in God also disbelieve in the existence of all other gods—usually by dismissing them rather than disproving them—it is incumbent upon the person who believes in one god to engage the problem of the existence of many other gods. One cannot therefore debate that the God of Abraham, Isaac, and Jacob exists but simply ignore the debate over the existence of Zeus, Thor, or Baal. The honest person, faced with the enormous task of proving or disproving the existence of every possible god, may well abandon the quest to prove even the one he prefers.

The apologetic illustrates that the core question in modern understandings of religion is *belief in God,* that is, whether one agrees with the assertion that God exists. If one does not believe in the existence of God or gods, then one can justifiably reject everything else that goes with religion—prayer, worship, clergy, temples, churches, doctrine, holidays, etc.

I bring this up not to launch into a proof for the existence of God or reasons why we should dismiss all other gods' existence without disproof (I will leave those tasks to others if needed), but rather to show that the way we tend to think about religion in the twenty-first century has been sharply reduced. "Do you believe in the existence of god or gods?" is not a question that ancient people engaged with. By asking this question, we assume categories that would have been

3 Stephen F. Roberts, "Brief History of the Quote," Ask Atheists, https://www.askatheists.com/user/5972.

alien to the ancient people among whom the oldest religions arose. Nevertheless, when modern people look back at most of human history, we tend to categorize religion according to this question. So we may feel befuddled when we don't find an answer to that question in the relevant religious texts.

The Christian, for instance, looking to prove that Yahweh exists, will not find an argument for His existence in the Bible. The closest he or she might get to an apologetic against atheism is Psalm 14:1: "The fool says in his heart, 'There is no God.' / They are corrupt, they do abominable deeds; / there is none who does good." Despite being used often against atheists, that verse is not a proof for God's existence, and an atheist would find it only an insult. But, as we shall see, the verse is not about atheism at all, since atheism was not an argument anyone was making at the time. Why, then, is the existence of the divine the peg on which we so often hang our discussion of religion? It is because that question defines the models we are using. So what models are we actually using?

Monotheism and Polytheism

Modern discourse generally recognizes three categories of religion: monotheist, polytheist, and nontheist. In the first category, we find Christianity, Rabbinic Judaism, and Islam (as well as a few others), which believe in one God. In the second are most of the varieties of paganism and (depending on how you define it) Hinduism, which have many gods. In the third are religions like Buddhism, which is said to be nontheist.[4] These categories answer the question, "How

4 Buddhism as a family of religious traditions does not have a creator deity, but nonetheless believes in elevated beings which are referred to with divine language and who are venerated with practices that fit many definitions of worship, such as offerings of food and incense. Thus, including Buddhism in the category of nontheist religion is problematic. I mention it here, though, because it is usually classified this way.

many gods are there?" And if something is a god, then it is worthy of our worship. So the doctrine of belief in the divine is inseparable from the worship of it.

But monotheism, polytheism, and nontheism are not categories that the people who practiced these religions would have recognized for most of human history. And it is not even a traditionally Christian set of categories, though most Christians nowadays would recognize and affirm them. One cannot find a doctrine of monotheism versus polytheism in the Bible, arguing that one God exists and other gods do not.

Although I have mentioned other religions above such as Judaism and Buddhism, my focus in this book is not generally on world religions[5] but rather on Christianity, so I will leave aside these other traditions with a significant exception—paganism. But why would we look at paganism? Because the world in which the faith of Abraham, Isaac, and Jacob arose, in which Moses led Israel out of Egypt, into which Jesus was born, and into which the apostles were sent out to preach was pagan. We see this pagan context witnessed throughout the Bible, with references to the nations who worshiped Baal, Zeus, and other gods. Israel interacts with ancient Near Eastern paganism throughout the Old Testament, and the Church's primary growth in the New Testament is from Greek and Roman pagans.

The language of the Scriptures, including the language of its prayers, is often incomprehensible without this pagan context. If we have no sense of paganism and its gods, how can we understand what God means when He says He will judge the gods of Egypt (Ex. 12:12; Num. 33:4) or that He is above all gods (1 Chron. 16:25; Ps. 95:3,

5 If you're interested in my analysis of other religions, especially other varieties of Christianity as compared with Orthodox Christianity, see my book *Orthodoxy and Heterodoxy: Finding the Way to Christ in a Complicated Religious Landscape* (Ancient Faith Publishing, 2017).

96:4, 97:9, 135:5)? Why does God command Israel to make no covenants with other gods (Ex. 23:32)? Or what can St. Paul mean when he forbids the Corinthian Christians from participating in pagan sacrifices because they put one into communion with demons (1 Cor. 10:20–21)? From these and many other examples, we can see that the Scriptures not only reference pagan worship but even assume the true existence of the gods of the pagans. The model of monotheism versus polytheism—belief in one god versus many gods—falls apart when we begin to look at the language Scripture uses for the gods of the nations.

But what about passages that refer to Yahweh as the "true" God (2 Chron. 15:3; Jer. 10:10, etc.) and the gods of the nations as "false" gods (Jer. 14:22, 18:15) who even "are not gods" (2 Chron. 13:9; Gal. 4:8)? If we take these passages to mean "Yahweh exists and the other gods do not," then we see a contradiction with the many other passages that treat the gods of the nations as actual entities. But the contradiction is only apparent and is borne of our modern sense that the main question about a god is whether it exists or not. So what is going on here?

What Does god *Mean?*

Etymology is not the only way to understand what words mean and can often be misleading when a word has moved beyond its historical origins. But in the case of the words used for *god* in the Christian Scriptures, we need to pay this some attention. In the Hebrew of the Bible, the word for "god" is *el* (plural *elohim*). As far as linguists know, from its most ancient proto-Semitic roots, this word has referred to spiritual beings. And there is not one word for the God of Israel and another for the gods of the nations—they are both called *el*. There is also not one word for imaginary gods and another for real ones. So if we call the nations' deities "false gods," then we might think they are imaginary, but this is not the case.

To find a clue as to why "false gods" does not mean imaginary beings, let's look at the Greek of the Bible, both in the ancient Jewish translation of the Old Testament and also in the New Testament. Throughout the Greek Bible, the word for "god" is *theos* (plural *theoi*). Its Proto-Indo-European roots reach back to a term meaning "to do, to put, to place." From there, we see the word being applied to people, especially rulers, who put things into place. Thus, the sense of *theos* is derived from rulership. The gods are the ultimate rulers, the ones who organize things at the highest level.

Although the Bible was not written in English, since we are English speakers, it's worth looking at the origin of the English word *god*, as well. Its origins are also Indo-European, and it comes from a verb meaning "to call upon, to invoke." Thus, the history of the English word *god* is bound up with prayer (in its most basic sense, *prayer* is simply "asking"). We don't usually think of the word *god* that way anymore, but of course the idea of calling upon a god in prayer is part of our concept of divinity. And if gods are rulers, then calling upon them only makes sense. Listening to petitions is part of what rulers do.

So with all this in mind, let's return to some of our biblical expressions that seem to speak of the nonexistence of pagan gods. To refer to a god-as-ruler as "false" thus means that he is a usurper. He's not really in charge. To say that he "is no god" is not to say that he doesn't exist but rather to say that he's a pretender occupying a position that doesn't belong to him.

Let's look again at Psalm 14:1: "The fool says in his heart, 'There is no God.' / They are corrupt, they do abominable deeds; / there is none who does good." Since there were no atheists in the ancient world, the fool saying to himself, "There is no God" is not denying God's existence. Rather, he is saying, "No one is in charge." He engages in evil deeds because he thinks no one is watching over him. That is why the next verse reads, "The Lord looks down from heaven on the children of man, / to see if there are any who understand, / who seek after God" (Ps. 14:2).

We can also understand why the Romans often executed early Christians by charging them with atheism. In that ancient conception, "atheism" didn't mean "they don't believe in any god." The Romans knew full well that Christians worshiped their own God. Rather, they were calling Christians unruly. The Romans were saying that Christians did not recognize and submit to the rulers of the Romans—Jupiter and the Roman pantheon, which included Caesar as one of the gods. They were saying that Christians were rebels.

Once we understand this concept of a god as a ruler, then we can understand the language the Bible uses about the gods of the nations, and we can see that these various passages that both acknowledge the gods' existence and also call them "false" do not actually contradict each other. More importantly, we can see why one of the most frequent commandments God gave to His people is this: worship Him alone. The threat from paganism is not a problem of people believing in fairy-tale beings that are made-up. The threat is that God's people would turn away from worshiping Him and communing with Him to worship and therefore commune with deities that St. Paul and other biblical writers identify as demons.

But we should not simply map the word *god* in our minds to the word *demon* and see every use of *god* in the Bible or the rest of Christian tradition as a reference to the demonic gods of the nations. It turns out that the Bible uses *god* in four different ways.

How Is god *Used in the Bible?*

We have already seen how the Hebrew and Greek of the Bible use their respective words for *god* to mean "spiritual being" and "ruler." But as I said earlier, etymology isn't everything when it comes to understanding the meaning of words. A particular passage might use *god* to refer to the pagan demonic deities without acknowledgment that they really are (or ought to be) rulers. Indeed, much of the Bible's apologetic against pagan gods is that they are incapable of doing what they claim (which we will discuss later). So let's turn now to the actual beings to which the Bible applies the word *god*, which we can divide into four general categories.

First of all, in its truest, best, fullest, most correct sense, *god* is applied to the God of Abraham, Isaac, and Jacob, Yahweh the God of Israel, the Father, Son, and Holy Spirit. He is often referred to in the Old Testament with the plural form *Elohim*, which does not mean that He is "gods." Rather, it is a plural of intensity, meaning roughly "God of all gods," that He is the most "God" that any god can be.[6] In the Greek translation of the Old Testament and in the Greek of the New Testament, *Theos* gets used in this same way. Whenever you see *God* with a capital G in English Bibles, it's usually a translation of one of these two words.

Second, we also see *gods* used in the Bible for the spiritual beings that pagan nations worshiped. A few examples will suffice: "You shall have no other gods before me" (Ex. 20:3), "You shall make no covenant with them and their gods" (Ex. 23:32), and "You shall not go after other gods, the gods of the peoples who are around you" (Deut. 6:14). We also see *gods* referring to the idolatrous images the pagan nations used in their worship, such as the many references to gods made of wood, stone, bronze, iron, silver, and gold (e.g., Deut. 4:28; Dan. 5:4; Ex. 20:23). We can see that the Scriptures take the evil gods

6 Hebrew plurals are used this way in other contexts, such as for the demon *Behemoth*, a plural form with a singular meaning of "beast of all beasts," the most beastly beast that is possible. Sometimes this form gets confusingly translated as a plural in English, such as in Ex. 32:4, "These are your gods, O Israel, who brought you up out of the land of Egypt!" The word there is *Elohim*, and Aaron is pointing at a single idol. He is not saying that gods (plural) brought Israel out of Egypt, but rather that the people will now use the golden calf idolatrously to try to worship the God of gods (that is, Yahweh).

of the nations very seriously—they are real, and the pagans worship them through the use of idols.

These first two uses of *god* are probably not very surprising, and we are used to them because they conform to the monotheism/polytheism model of thinking about religion. A closer look at the biblical usage of *god* can lead us into unfamiliar territory, however, starting with the third category.

The Bible calls angels "gods." Yet aren't we supposed to worship God alone? That is true, but if we set aside the assumption that *god* refers to a being that one must worship (remember that the basic sense means "ruler"), then we can see that this usage isn't a problem. But does the Bible really call angels "gods"? Yes, it does. In numerous places, the Bible says that God is greater than all other gods (Ex. 18:11; 1 Chron. 16:25; 2 Chron. 2:5; Ps. 95:3, 97:9, 135:5) and that other gods are commanded to bow to God (Deut. 32:43; Ps. 97:7). We might interpret these as the pagan gods being told to repent and submit to God, but that interpretation doesn't work if we consider this language: "Give thanks to the God of gods, / for his steadfast love endures forever" (Ps. 136:2). The psalm is not calling Him the God of pagan gods! We can find similar language in the mouths of the prophets Moses (Deut. 10:17) and Daniel (Dan. 11:36). These prophets, speaking for God (respectively) to Israel and to the Babylonian king, would not declare God to be the ruler of wicked spiritual beings—such would be unbecoming language. Rather, this language refers to the spiritual beings we generally call angels: the gods who bow to Him and accompany Him in service.

The concept of the angels as gods is shocking if we assume the monotheism/polytheism model. But we have already seen that that model does not work with the Scriptures. And we have also seen that just because something is a god does not mean that it ought to be worshiped. Saint Paul is clear that we are not to worship angels

(Col. 2:18), and according to St. John, angels do not accept worship (Rev. 22:8–9).

So when we look at how the Scriptures use the word *god,* we see that there is Yahweh the God of Israel and that there are also many other gods. Some of these gods disobey God—the gods of the nations. Some remain obedient—the angels. If *god* means "ruler" or "spiritual being," then angels certainly qualify, as spiritual beings to whom God has delegated some of His rule through their obedient ministry.

The Bible applies the word *god* to a fourth (and possibly most shocking) category—human beings. In 1 Samuel 28, we read the famous incident where Saul goes to a witch to summon up the spirit of the dead prophet Samuel. When the spirit comes up out of the ground, the witch declares "I see a god coming up out of the earth" (1 Sam. 28:13). The rest of the chapter treats this spirit truly as the prophet Samuel. Nowhere does it say that this god is some other spirit; instead, it says, for instance, that Samuel speaks in verses 14 and 15, and that the words he says are from the Lord, prophesying correctly what will happen to Saul and to Israel.

The Bible uses the word *god* in another important way to refer to humans. In John 10:34–36, Christ says:

> Is it not written in your Law, "I said, you are gods"? If he called them gods to whom the word of God came—and Scripture cannot be broken—do you say of him whom the Father consecrated and sent into the world, "You are blaspheming," because I said, "I am the Son of God"?

What does this mean, "He called them gods"? This passage can be understood in several ways, but this elaboration from St. Theophylact of Ohrid will illustrate my point: "Now, they are called gods, *unto whom the Word of God came,* but the name *Word of God* refers to Me. I dwelt in those who are called gods and graciously adopted them as sons; therefore, I am justly called God, more than any one of them. I am God by nature, and I bestow divinity upon others."[7]

Here we see a new use of *god,* something more than "spiritual being" or "ruler." Jesus says that those in whom He dwells can be called "gods" through adoption as His sons when He bestows His divinity upon them. As with angels (either obedient or fallen), that does not mean they are equal to God or should be worshiped, but it does mean that they become closely associated with Christ, who is Himself God. This bestowal of divinity from God is traditionally referred to by the Greek word *theosis.*

Finally, we should refer to one more saying from Jesus who, in Luke 20:36, says that the "sons of the resurrection" are "equal to angels" and are "sons of God." We will discuss this more later, but it should suffice for now to note that human beings who are in Christ, as God's "sons" and "equal to angels," are therefore rightly called gods.

How Is God Different from the gods?

Even though we have seen that only Yahweh the God of Israel is worthy of worship, those who hold to the monotheism/polytheism model of thinking worry that using *god* to refer to anyone else must mean these other beings ought to be worshiped, that the gods are equal to God. We know, however, that the Bible does in fact use the word *god* to refer to angels, pagan deities, and humans. But this does not need to be a problem because the Bible also constantly reminds us that Yahweh is totally different from all the other gods:

---

7 Theophylact, *The Explanation of the Holy Gospel According to John* (House Springs, MO: Chrysostom Press, 2007), 173.

> "Who is like you, O LORD, among the gods? / Who is like you, majestic in holiness, / awesome in glorious deeds, doing wonders?" (Ex. 15:11)

> "The house that I am to build will be great, for our God is greater than all gods." (2 Chron. 2:5)

> There is none like you among the gods, O Lord, / nor are there any works like yours. (Ps. 86:8)

> For the LORD is a great God, / and a great King above all gods. (Ps. 95:3)

> For You, O LORD, are most high over all the earth; / you are exalted far above all gods. (Ps. 97:9)

That the God of Israel is unlike any other "gods" and greater than all of them is apparent everywhere in Scripture. Even the name of His chief archangel—Michael, one of the gods—is a rhetorical question, since the name Michael means "who is like God?" Psalm 86:8 gives the answer: no one.

Further, in many places the Bible uses comparative, relative titles for God that show how He is different from the other gods, the lesser spiritual beings that He created. Among such titles is *Lord of Hosts*—in Hebrew, *Yahweh Sabaoth*[8]—which is used hundreds of times, a title referring to God as the commander of the armies of heaven. We

8 Despite what some scholars might say, *Yahweh Sabaoth* does not mean "Lord of the Sabbath." *Sabbath* in Hebrew is *Shabath*, whereas *Sabaoth* is from the Hebrew *tzabha* (plural *tzabhaoth*), which means "army." In the Greek Old Testament, this same phrase is translated as *Kyrios Dynameon*, "Lord of Powers." In the Divine Liturgy of the Orthodox Church, during the anaphora, this phrase often gets rendered "Lord of Sabaoth," referencing Is. 6:3: "Holy, holy, holy, Lord of Sabaoth, heaven and earth are full of His glory."

also see *God of gods* and *Lord of lords,* as well as *King of kings*. One might interpret these latter two as referring to God's lordship over earthly rulers, but *God of gods* means that He is greater than and ruler over all gods.

Most interestingly, God is called *Most High God* or simply *Most High* in dozens of places. If He is the most high, then there must be other gods. But didn't pagans have a concept of a "most high god"? They did, and usually this most high god was a king or father over the rest, just as Yahweh is. Pagan figures such as Zeus, Odin, Dievas, or Ra are the most high gods of their pantheons. So how is this title different when applied to the God of Israel?

First, as told in their own stories, almost none of the pagan most high gods permanently hold that position. Zeus, for instance, is the third to hold that title in Greek mythology, succeeding his father Kronos, who himself succeeded his own father Ouranos—and these successions came from violent coups. Such succession myths are common throughout pagan mythology, with a most high god installed by deposing a previous one.

By contrast, when the Bible tells the same story, the insurrection fails:

> "How you are fallen from heaven,
> O Day Star, son of Dawn!
> How you are cut down to the ground,
> you who laid the nations low!
> You said in your heart,
> 'I will ascend to heaven;
> above the stars of God
> I will set my throne on high;
> I will sit on the mount of assembly
> in the far reaches of the north;

I will ascend above the heights of the clouds;
  I will make myself like the Most High.'
But you are brought down to Sheol,
  to the far reaches of the pit." (Is. 14:12–15)

The "Day Star, son of Dawn" here is the devil, one of the angels who sought to exalt himself to be like the Most High. Yet he is cast down to Sheol, the underworld of death. In the Scriptures, the Most High God is eternally in that high place. There was never any before Him, nor will there be any after Him. The eternality of God's rule above all gods is unlike any of the pagan stories of their most high gods.

The other key way that the Bible distinguishes God from the gods is in capability. Psalm 86:8 says that none of the works of the gods is like the works of God. The Bible goes further than that, though, when addressing the rebellious pagan gods, and constantly calls them totally weak and incapable. When the Bible calls these gods "false," it means that they are weak: "Are there any among the false gods of the nations that can bring rain? / Or can the heavens give showers? / Are you not he, O Lord our God? / We set our hope on you, / for you do all these things" (Jer. 14:22). This incapability contrasts with God, who is therefore the "true" God: "But the Lord is the true God; / he is the living God and the everlasting King. / At his wrath the earth quakes, / and the nations cannot endure his indignation. Thus shall you say to them: 'The gods who did not make the heavens and the earth shall perish from the earth and from under the heavens'" (Jer. 10:10–11).

The apologetic for the capability of God finds its full expression in the Scripture's emphasis on God as the Creator of all things. Pagan creation stories include gods (sometimes the most high god, but not always) who make things, but not in terms of true creation in the sense of making something out of nothing. Pagan creation myths are about gods rearranging existing things into new things. Often, creation is made out of the body of another god or a giant, or it might be birthed from a mother goddess. But however it is depicted, these mythologies do not claim that the creator gods have made all things. Thus, a major differentiation that the Scriptures make for God is that He is the universal Creator. The Bible says, in many places, that God has made all things (Is. 44:24; Jer. 10:16, 51:19; John 1:3). He is the maker of heaven and earth (Gen. 1:1; 2 Kgs. 19:15; Is. 51:13), and it all belongs to Him and He rules over it (Deut. 10:14; Josh. 2:11; 1 Chron. 29:11).

We also see the weakness of the pagan gods in that they can be bribed and God cannot: "For the Lord your God is God of gods and Lord of lords, the great, the mighty, and the awesome God, who is not partial and takes no bribe" (Deut. 10:17). According to their own myths, the pagan gods have needs—for sacrifices, for pleasure, for power, for prestige, etc. Through idolatry, mortals meet those needs and hope to get something back in exchange—good weather, fertility, beauty, victory in war, etc. Scripture says both that the pagan gods cannot deliver on their promises and that God does not need anything.

All these themes come together in St. Paul's apologetic to the pagan philosophers of Athens on the Areopagus: "The God who made the world and everything in it, being Lord of heaven and earth, does not live in temples made by man, nor is he served by human hands, as though he needed anything, since he himself gives to all mankind life and breath and everything" (Acts 17:24–25). What makes God different from the pagan gods? He created all things, which makes Him stronger than all gods and in need of nothing. By contrast, the pagan gods crave the worship of humankind but can't even accomplish what they promise, because they are creations themselves who don't even have the courage to claim to have created everything.

The final difference between God and the gods is that He loves humankind as the height and purpose of His creation. A survey of the myths of paganism reveals that the gods do not love human beings. When they're not raping or otherwise exploiting humanity, pitting us against each other, they often don't even notice us.

In the Bible, the pinnacle of Creation occurs when the one God makes humans. In pagan creation myths, however, humans are often a kind of afterthought or even an accident or side effect, sometimes a group project by some of the gods and not always even the most important ones. In Greek myth, a lesser god called Prometheus makes humanity; he shapes humans out of mud, and Athena breathes life into them. In Norse myth, Odin and his brothers either stumbled upon the first humans or use a tree to form them. In Egyptian myth, Ra's eye gets separated from him, and in the struggle to get it back, tears are shed, which become humankind. In Baltic myth, humanity results when Dievas coughs and spits, and his saliva lands in fertile soil—the god didn't even notice it had happened.[9]

Pagan religions conceive their gods as the biggest and most powerful beings in the world rather than as an omnipotent Creator who needs nothing. The God who made all things and made humankind to be the height of His creation, who does not need anything from us and takes no bribe, who then gives to us not only life but also sustenance, enters into a relationship with us freely. He needs nothing from us, so everything He does for us is an act of love. No pagan god ever did any of that.

All this, therefore, is why God is rightly called the *Lord of Spirits*. He is their Creator and their King, their Commander and the One who is

9 These are some versions of these various mythologies' creation myths. One can find a lot of variation on all these points in the extant sources.

above them all. He is not like any created thing, for He made them all Himself. He is the Uncreated.

In Scripture, then, we do not see an image of only one divine being—God—with the rest cast aside as imaginary fairy tales. Rather, the world of Israel and of the pagans is one world, filled with spiritual beings called *gods*. In the pagan conception, one god rules the rest by force and could be deposed, with many gods each pursuing their own desires and sometimes dragging humans along with them, usually to their destruction. Humans in relationship with the gods encounter dangerous beings who could turn on them on a whim.

In the biblical image, the true God and ruler over all is present among the hosts of heaven, the many gods, the angels who either serve Him or rebel against Him. God created humanity out of love, and while the rebellious gods seek to destroy humanity, the obedient ones assist God in His ministry to us.

CHAPTER 2

Angels and Demons

Now there was a day when the sons of God came to present themselves before the Lord, *and Satan also came among them.*

—Job 1:6

On the right hand and on the left hand of God, then, stands the Angelic Host, forasmuch as both the will of the elect spirits harmonizes with Divine mercy, and the mind of the reprobate, in serving their own evil ends, obeys the judgment of His strict decrees.

—St. Gregory the Dialogist[1]

Whether they refer to them as "gods" (we saw in the previous chapter that the Bible does), Christians believe in angels and demons. Orthodox and other Christians confess in the

1 Saint Gregory the Dialogist, *Moralia in Job* (n.p.: Lectionary Central, n.d.), 2.38, http://www.lectionarycentral.com/GregoryMoralia/Book02.html.

Nicene Creed: "We believe in one God, the Father almighty, Maker of heaven and earth and of all things visible and invisible." It is thus an ancient Christian dogma that creation includes invisible things, and what we primarily mean when we refer to the invisible creation is that we believe in angels and demons.

Likewise, nearly every religion throughout the world in some way believes in angels and demons. Throughout all of human history, we have felt the presence of unseen, intelligent spiritual beings—some good, some evil—who influence our world and interact with it in some way. Depictions abound of these spiritual beings in both art and literature, showing numerous encounters both on the periphery of human senses and unmistakably face-to-face.

Most Christians in the modern period believe that these spirits are not just on the periphery of what we can sense, but we go so far as to marginalize them in terms of conscious regard. We see angels as helpers whom God has sent to assist us in our Christian life but who are not actually central to salvation itself. They're part of the spiritual world, yet we feel they are optional in day-to-day Christian life. But as we will see in a later chapter, angels are actually central to how the Bible presents salvation.

Likewise, demons are also out on the margins. They try to get in the way of Christian life, but they are not actually primarily responsible for the state humankind is in, the very reason we need salvation to begin with. Yet demons were involved in every aspect of the Fall of humankind and instigated it—the introduction of death, the proliferation of sin, and our domination by these dark powers.[2] Further, the Bible describes Christ's whole mission as about destroying the

2 The devil tempts Adam and Eve, and they receive death. Sin is a demonic force that overwhelms Cain and then spreads through the civilization he founds. Demons later dominate humankind through idolatry. See my book *Arise, O God* (Ancient Faith Publishing, 2021) for a fuller account of this demonic involvement.

works of the devil (1 John 3:8). So with this marginalization in mind, let's try to recover a fuller image of how these spirits figure into the Christian life.

Who Are the Angels?

The first question we usually ask about strange subjects is, "What is it?" In this case, what is an angel? But this way of knowing things is not congruent with most of human experience, which begins with encounter, not analysis and definition. So I want to start not with the "what" but rather the "who": who are the angels? (Since demons are fallen angels, we will get to that later.)

As mentioned in the previous chapter, the Scriptures call God *Lord of Hosts*—hundreds of times, in fact. The angels are these hosts. *Hosts* is a military term, meaning that the angels are God's armies. Since He is the Lord of Hosts, to encounter God is also to encounter His hosts.

We first unmistakably encounter angels when God appears to Abraham at Mamre:

> And the Lord appeared to him by the oaks of Mamre, as he sat at the door of his tent in the heat of the day. He lifted up his eyes and looked, and behold, three men were standing in front of him. When he saw them, he ran from the tent door to meet them and bowed himself to the earth and said, "O Lord, if I have found favor in your sight, do not pass by your servant." (Gen. 18:1–3)

Some interpret the three men that Abraham sees as the Father, Son, and Holy Spirit. After all, there are three of them, and the chapter begins with saying that it was "the Lord" who appeared. Further, Abraham bows in front of them and says, "O Lord." But a visible appearance of the Father and the Spirit in the form of men would be extremely strange compared to all other theophanies in Scripture. Nowhere else in Scripture do we see the Father appearing as a man except perhaps in certain prophetic visions such as in Daniel or in Revelation, but never does the Holy Spirit manifest this way. Yet we do not need to conjecture because the beginning of the next chapter identifies two of these men explicitly as angels who go down to Sodom to see Abraham's nephew Lot (Gen. 19:1). The rest of the chapter describes how these angels rescue Lot and his family from the destruction that God sends to Sodom because of the city's great sins.

We can see from this encounter that angels can appear in the form of men, that they accompany God, and that they do His works. On that first point—their appearance—I think it's worth noting that, despite what you may see on the internet about "biblically accurate angels" (usually accompanied by images of winged wheels with a myriad of eyes), angels typically present themselves to humans as men (usually young men). The bizarre depictions that we see in some prophetic visions are also legitimate experiences, but they are not the way angels ordinarily look when humans see them. Why might this be? When humans have visions of angels, it is not an arbitrary display of God's power, nor is it for the purpose of having an esoteric spiritual experience. Rather, God sends angels to humans to minister to them. So if they appear to us as something like ourselves, we are more likely to accept them. (We will discuss whether they really have bodies below.)

Another encounter with angels from the Old Testament especially worth mentioning here is not actually documented in the text itself; rather, we see it in an icon. At the ancient Orthodox Monastery of the Transfiguration at the foot of Mount Sinai (commonly known as St. Katherine's), there is an icon of Moses at Sinai, showing various scenes. The top of the icon shows Moses on the mountain and God handing him the tablets of the Torah (Law), but not directly. Angels are passing them to Moses from God. However, the account of this event in Exodus does not mention angels. So where did the iconographer get this idea? Did he make it up? Actually, the New Testament mentions the Torah coming through angels (Acts 7:53; Gal. 3:19; Heb. 2:2), a detail we may miss if we read these verses without a sense of their relation to the Exodus account. The apostles didn't make up this detail, either, but simply repeated the tradition they had received as part of Israel. It was such an important tradition that St. Stephen included it in the sermon he preached as he was about to be martyred (Acts 7:53).

The belief that angels gave the Torah to Moses is also represented in an extra-biblical Jewish text from the second century BC, the Book of Jubilees.[3] In chapter 2, a figure referred to as the "angel of the presence" encounters Moses on Sinai and tells him the story of Creation and commands him to write it down.[4] It is clear that this angel is not the Son of God (the Angel of the Lord) because he often refers to himself with the other angels as "we," speaking of what he saw God doing in Creation.

Why bring up this encounter with angels? First, it shows that encounters with God often take place in the midst of the multitude of the heavenly hosts. But it also shows that angelic ministry to us is precisely God's ministry. It is not something separate but is God acting through them. He does not need them. He could have made the Torah appear in Moses' hands or made the tablets appear in the mountainside like they do in Cecil B. DeMille's film *The Ten Commandments.* He shares His ministry with the angels because of His love for them.

---

3 For details on how the Orthodox Church has read and used books like Jubilees, Enoch, etc., see Fr. Stephen De Young's book *Apocrypha: An Introduction to Extra-Biblical Literature* (Ancient Faith Publishing, 2023).

4 Jubilees, in *The Old Testament Pseudepigrapha,* ed. James H. Charlesworth, vol. 2 (Peabody, MA: Hendrickson Publishers, 1983), 55.

Angels in the Life of Christ

When the Lord of Hosts Himself appears on earth and dwells among humanity—the Son of God, Jesus Christ—we should expect that angels will be at hand, accompanying Him and doing His works. Indeed, there is an archangel present at the very moment of the Incarnation itself, when God is made manifest as man, the beginning of His great work of salvation on this earth.

The archangel Gabriel appears in Luke 1:26–38, and in this passage, he fulfills the function of the word *angel*. The English word *angel* comes from the Greek *angelos,* a word that literally translates the Hebrew word *mal'ak*. Both the Greek and Hebrew mean "messenger." Although we often treat it that way, *angel* is not the name of a species but of a function. Humans encounter angels most frequently in the Scriptures as messengers, and the feast that celebrates the archangel's message to the Virgin Mary is called *Evangelismos* in Greek, which is usually translated "Annunciation" in English but literally refers to this act of bringing good news, the *evangelion*. Angels are thus messengers bringing the gospel.

Angels appear as messengers in Christ's Nativity as well, such as in Luke 2:8–15, where one begins speaking with the shepherds, and eventually a multitude of them appears, a "heavenly host" singing praises to God and His love. The identification of this host as "heavenly" is not mere poetry. Angels are associated with stars and the heavenly bodies throughout the Scriptures, and most notably in this case, there is one other time that the stars are described as singing, in Job 38:7, when at the creation of the world "the morning stars sang together / and all the sons of God shouted for joy." The message the angels deliver is on the same level as the creation of the world itself.

Angels also minister to Christ, caring for His physical needs and strengthening Him in two different scenes in the Gospels: after the devil tempts Him (Matt. 4:11; Mark 1:13) and when He is in agony in Gethsemane (Luke 22:43). These encounters reveal that angels not only deliver messages but also that they bring God's providential care. We see angels showing similar care to others, such as the prophet Elijah in 1 Kings 19:5–8, when an angel brings him food in the wilderness.

Angels fulfill their role as messengers when they deliver the most critical message relating to the life of Jesus: Christ is risen. This message is so crucial that all four Gospels record it (Matt. 28:1–10; Mark 16:1–8; Luke 24:1–9; John 20:11–18). In Matthew and Mark's Gospels, the angel tells the women entering Christ's empty Tomb not to be afraid. They are seeking Jesus who was crucified, but He is not there because He is risen. The angel then sends the women to go and tell Jesus' disciples what has happened. In Luke's account, two angels are present and deliver the memorable line, "Why do you seek the living among the dead?" They then remind the women how Christ had prophesied what would happen. The women then go tell the disciples what they saw. Finally, in John's Gospel, two angels speak to St. Mary Magdalene, asking her why she is weeping. She then sees the risen Christ herself, and she goes to tell the disciples that she has seen the Lord.

In all four Gospels, the message is the same: Christ is risen. And in all four Gospels, those who receive this message from the angelic messengers become *angeloi* themselves, messengers passing on the news that Jesus Christ is risen from the dead. The encounter with the messengers extends the gospel ministry from angels to humans.

The Ranks of Angels

We've spoken so far about angels and archangels, and these are the ranks of angels that humans encounter directly in the Scriptures. The Orthodox Tradition commonly presents nine ranks of angels—cherubim, seraphim, thrones, dominions, virtues, powers, principalities, archangels, and angels.[5] Generally, the highest ranks are those closest to God's throne, the second highest govern and act in the heavenly places, while the lowest ranks interact with humanity directly on earth. The imagery is of closeness or distance from God, but we should not understand this in materially spatial terms but rather as from the perspective of humankind's experience. God remains everywhere in creation, yet we still conceive of Him as "high" and ourselves as "low."[6]

We'll briefly discuss these ranks of angels, but first it's important to note that they are precisely *ranks*. These are not "kinds" of angels and certainly not species. As mentioned earlier, *angel* means "messenger," and these ranks also refer to functions that these spiritual beings carry out in obedience to God. Let's begin with the highest three ranks of angels, which are all associated with God's throne.

The highest two ranks, *cherubim* and *seraphim*, are what ancient religion called "throne guardians." The most high god is on his throne, and there are angelic beings standing around the throne who give protection but also serve as councilors. This image mirrors what one would see in a human court, with the king surrounded by bodyguards. In the tradition of the Scriptures, the Most High God of course does not need protection. Rather, these angels guard His throne in the sense that they guard humans *from* the throne. Why would they do that?

Throughout the Scriptures, we see that when sinful humans approach God, especially in a careless way, the contact can harm

5 This list appears explicitly in the *Celestial Hierarchy* of St. Dionysius the Areopagite, in the anaphora of the Divine Liturgy of St. Basil the Great, and in the liturgical texts for the feast of the angels on November 8. The lists, as well as how each rank is understood, can vary from source to source.

6 We will explore sacred cosmology more thoroughly in chapter 4.

them.[7] That is why so much of the religion of ancient Israel, and indeed of the Christian Church, is about purification, so that humans can prepare to meet God. But while that purification is absent or still in process, guardians prevent humans from accessing God's presence, precisely to keep them safe. The Scriptures set up this pattern in Genesis 3:24, where God places a cherub at the door to Paradise—the place where God dwelled on earth with humans—to prevent Adam and Eve from returning.

So if cherubim and seraphim both guard the throne, what is the difference between them? Before we address that, we should note that both images of throne guardians are shared with pagan religions in the ancient Near East, which is the setting for the Bible. Did Israel steal these figures from pagans, then? That question makes sense only if you assume that cherubim and seraphim appear just in stories that get passed between people. But the Bible treats them as real, so just as Israel experienced the same material world that pagans did, they experienced the same spiritual world. That world included these spiritual throne guardians, but as we just said, Israel's Most High God did not need them to guard *Him* like the pagan most high gods needed for their own thrones. So they agreed with pagans that these beings existed, but they disagreed on how they functioned.

The only real difference between cherubim and seraphim is how the Scriptures and the religious imagery from the region depict them. Cherubim are usually winged lions with human faces, and the image originates in Babylonian paganism. We see this image elsewhere in the region with some variations, such as the sphinx in Egypt, which

7 On *The Lord of Spirits* podcast, we call this "death by holiness." Some examples include Lev. 10:1–11, where God strikes down Nadab and Abihu, the sons of Aaron, after they enter the tabernacle to offer incense while drunk; St. Paul's warning that communing the Eucharist unworthily can lead to sickness or death (1 Cor. 11:27–32); or Acts 5:1–11, where Ananias and Sapphira lie to God and die.

does not have wings. The image continued into Christian art and produced the gryphon, which is well-known in medieval European Christianity. The Scriptures mention cherubim in many places, mostly referencing the art and statuary in the tabernacle, which God commanded. They also appear in visions in Ezekiel 1 and 10, the "four living creatures" who each have different faces.

Seraphim originally were depicted as winged serpents, and the image comes from Egyptian paganism. If you can imagine the head-dress of the Pharaohs, in which the head looks like a cobra, you can see that the Egyptian king, who himself had a cultic[8] role in his religion, looks like a throne guardian, a son of Ra (or Re) the Egyptian sun god. In the period surrounding the Exodus, Pharaoh was considered to be a body of the deity Horus, son of Ra.[9] Over time, the Christian tradition, because of the association of serpents with the devil, made seraphim look less like snakes, and they took on a more fantastical depiction of numerous wings surrounding a face. In Isaiah 6:1–6, seraphim with wings and faces appear in Isaiah's heavenly vision.

Thrones (in Hebrew, *ophanim*, "wheels") are the third rank of angels, and texts and iconography often depict them as wheels, sometimes with wings. The visions of Ezekiel, mentioned above, describe them as "whirling wheels" that are "full of eyes all around" (Ez. 1:18, 10:12–13). An ancient silver coin found in Israel dated from the fourth century BC shows God sitting on a winged wheel.[10] It seems strange to describe thrones as being wheels. Why wheels? Unlike pagan deities, who are generally associated with a particular geographic territory or

---

8 *Cultic* traditionally refers simply to worship. It does not necessarily carry the negative sense of *cult* in popular modern usage.

9 At other periods, Horus was considered a son of Osiris, with various divine mothers at different times.

10 This coin is one in a series referred to as the *Yehud coinage*, which bear Aramaic inscriptions and were minted in Judea, likely during the Persian Achaemenid rule of the region, though perhaps in the later Ptolemaic period.

region, the God of Israel is "both in heaven and on earth" (Ps. 113:11, LXX), meaning that He is everywhere and not limited by any territory; all things are in His domain. Thus, God's throne is also everywhere, and an image of mobility expresses this truth—hence, wheels. The Scriptures also describe this mobile throne of God as a chariot.

We might think of the next four ranks of angels as God's "government." They engage in combat, manage creation, and extend God's authority over humankind. The first of these ranks is the *dominions* (or *dominations* or *lordships*), which are tasked with resisting evil spiritual powers. When we see angelic beings engaged in war against fallen angels, this is the rank of the dominions.

After the dominions comes the rank of *virtues* (or *authorities*). These angels govern the creation—the sun, moon, and stars but also every element of the inanimate world, such as the waters and winds. The close association of this rank of angels with the heavenly bodies in particular is why these spirits are called the "heavenly host." We tend to think of *heaven* as a word referring to a spiritual afterlife, but as a concept it traditionally includes both the sky and the place where divine beings live. While the Bible does not describe the creation of the virtues (or any other angels, in fact), Jubilees does include the creation of some of the angels in chapter 2, where it lists them off in terms of their creation-governing tasks:

> For on the first day he created the heavens, which are above, and the earth, and the waters and all of the spirits which minister before him: the angels of the presence, and the angels of sanctification, and the angels of the spirit of fire, and the angels of the spirit of the winds, and the angels of the spirit of the clouds and darkness and snow and hail and frost, and the angels of resoundings and thunder and lightning, and the angels of the spirits of cold and heat and winter and springtime and harvest and summer, and all of the spirits of his creatures which are

> in heaven and on earth. And (he created) the abysses and darkness—both evening and night—and light—both dawn and daylight—which he prepared in the knowledge of his heart. (Jub. 2:2)[11]

The pagan world interpreted these creation-governing spirits as gods to be worshiped, jealously guarding their territory. This belief is the origin of animism, which says that almost everything has a soul or spirit that can be worshiped. But in the Orthodox Christian Tradition, the spirits that govern creation do so in obedience to God, and we are not to worship them. The Bible includes commands against worshiping the stars and other heavenly bodies (Deut. 4:19), something that pagans did readily—almost every pagan tradition includes sun and moon gods, for instance.

Powers (sometimes *authorities*) and *principalities* (or *rulers*) are angelic spirits who rule over the nations. These angels are the "sons of God" according to which the borders of the nations were fixed (Deut. 32:8). Generally, this arrangement is associated with the dividing of the traditional seventy nations after the Tower of Babel (Gen. 10–11). In Orthodox icons of the Tower of Babel, one can sometimes see each of the nations, represented by men dressed in various national costumes, being accompanied by an angel as they depart. These angels were essentially patron saints of the nations, whom God sent to govern on His behalf.

The nations ended up worshiping these spirits, however, who accepted that worship and thereby fell into evil, cementing their enslavement of the nations through idolatry. The third-century Christian writer Lactantius witnessed this belief:

> The poets both know them to be demons, and so describe them. Hesiod thus speaks: "These are the demons according to the will of Zeus,

11 Jubilees, 55.

> Good, living on the earth, the guardians of mortal men." And this is said for this purpose, because God had sent them as guardians to the human race; but they themselves also, though they are the destroyers of men, yet wish themselves to appear as their guardians, that they themselves may be worshipped, and God may not be worshipped.[12]

In the Christian tradition, this is the origin of paganism. God later creates a new nation for Himself, Israel, and appoints the archangel Michael as its guardian. Since that time, patron saints (including unfallen angels) take up this role of guarding and governing the nations that the original powers and principalities abandoned.

The final two ranks of angels are the *archangels* and *angels*. These are the angelic spirits that directly interact most often with humankind, protecting us and delivering messages to us. These angels serve as the guardian angels who are traditionally assigned to each Christian at baptism. Guardian angels in particular are tasked with guiding the Christian on the path of righteousness and defending him or her from attacks by demonic spirits. Usually when you see an angel in the Scriptures, especially when no name is mentioned, it is an angel or archangel. As we saw earlier, *angel* means "messenger." *Archangel* means "chief angel."

Finally, there is another group of angels who are not part of the nine ranks—the *Seven Archangels*. These seven spirits, who are distinct from the rank called *archangels*, are mentioned in the Revelation of St. John (3:1, 4:5, 5:6, 8:2, 16:1); they stand before God's throne and are in a sense above all the others. They also appear in the Old

---

12 Lactantius, *Divine Institutes*, trans. William Fletcher, in *Ante-Nicene Fathers*, eds. Alexander Roberts, James Donaldson and A. Cleveland Coxe, vol. 7 (Peabody, MA: Hendrickson Publishers, 1999), 26–28.

Testament. In Zechariah 4:10, these seven are the "eyes of the LORD, which range through the whole earth," while in Tobit 12:15, the archangel Raphael identifies himself as one of these seven. They seem to stand apart from the nine ranks and sometimes function as one or another of them—sometimes delivering messages, sometimes guarding, sometimes battling against demons, and so on.

There are various lists of the names of the Seven Archangels. All of them share the same first three—Michael, Gabriel, and Raphael—because the Scriptures mention these three by name. The other four, as found in various sources, are Uriel, Selaphiel (or Salathiel), Jegudiel (or Jehudiel), and Barachiel. Names from other traditions for the Seven Archangels include Suriel, Camael, Jophiel, Zadkiel, Raguel, Sariel, Phanuel, Sachiel, Sarathiel, and Ananiel. There is sometimes an eighth, named Jerahmeel or Jeremiel.

Angels in Liturgical Encounter

Before we turn to the "What are the angels?" question, we should look at one final place of encounter—liturgical encounter. Perhaps the most familiar service to Orthodox Christians is the Divine Liturgy, and there are many references in its text to the angels. We will look at three from the beginning of the service. The first reference to angels in the Liturgy is in the prayer said by the priest before the Little Entrance: "O Master, Lord our God, who hast appointed in heaven orders and hosts of angels and archangels for the service of Thy glory: Cause that with our entrance there may be an entrance of holy angels serving with us and glorifying Thy goodness."[13] With this prayer, it is fully expected that angels will accompany the clergy through the

13 Quotations from the Divine Liturgy are taken from *The Liturgikon: The Book of Divine Services for the Priest and Deacon,* 4th ed. (Bolivar, PA: The Antiochian Orthodox Christian Archdiocese of America, 2021).

holy doors into the holy place as the Gospel book is processed in. This association of angels with the holy place where the altar sits comes, as we have seen, directly from the traditional understanding of angels serving in the presence of God. Immediately following the Little Entrance, the priest says the Prayer of the Thrice-Holy Hymn:

> O holy God, who restest in the holies, who art hymned by the seraphim with the thrice-holy cry and glorified by the cherubim and worshipped by every heavenly power . . . Thyself, O Master, receive even from the mouth of us sinners the thrice-holy hymn and visit us in Thy goodness.

The choir is about to sing the Trisagion (thrice-holy) Hymn, and the priest's prayer joins the singing of this hymn on earth to what the angels sing to the Lord of Hosts, as witnessed in Scripture (Is. 6:3). Toward the end of the thrice-holy hymn, the priest approaches the throne at the high place (behind the altar) and says: "Blessed is he that cometh in the name of the Lord. . . . Blessed art Thou on the throne of the glory of Thy kingdom, who art enthroned upon the cherubim."

The movement toward the throne of God is now complete and the Divine Liturgy proper may begin. All along the way, we are making this movement and singing along with the angels, and deeper in the text of the Divine Liturgy, at its very heart in the anaphora, we also see the angels mentioned. Why? Because angels accompany and assist our entrance into the holy place to offer up the sacrifice; they are indeed present there with us.

Other divine services mention angels frequently, but perhaps the best place to look is in the hymns for their feast day on November 8, which is especially dedicated to the archangels Michael and Gabriel. The following is a sample of a few of the hymns to St. Michael:

> With a dazzling bright radiance, thou, O Michael, dost stand before the Three-Sun Divinity with the Hosts on high, O Chief Commander, in joy exclaiming: Holy art Thou, O Lord, God the Father in the heights; Holy art Thou, the Word of God co-beginningless; Holy art Thou, Divine and Holy Spirit: one Divinity, one Power, one Glory, Nature, and Sovereignty.[14]

In this hymn, we see the relationship of the angels to God—standing before Him and praising the Holy Trinity. Here we see an elaboration on the thrice-holy hymn.

> Both thy visage is fiery, and thy beauty, astonishing; and since thou by nature art immaterial, thou dost traverse all the farthest parts, fulfilling the sovereign will of the Maker of all things, Michael, Chief of the Angels' Hosts, mighty in thy strength; and thou makest the temple honoured with thy holy name to be a well-spring of help and healings for maladies.

Here, the hymnographer describes the "fiery" appearance and beauty of the archangel, who is able because of his immateriality to travel throughout all creation. Further, churches named for him are the locus of healing.

> Thou Who makest Thy ministers flames of fire, as the Scripture saith, and Thine Angels spirits, O Lord, Thou hast shown forth as first among arch angelic ranks great Michael, the Chief of Hosts, who fulfilleth Thy commands with devoted obedience and who crieth out with a great voice the awesome and thrice-holy hymn of praise unto Thy glory with fear and trembling, O Word of God.

---

14 This and the following two hymns are from Great Vespers in the *November Menaion* (Brookline, MA: Holy Transfiguration Monastery, 2005).

Finally, the hymnographer repeats the fiery description from Scripture (Ps. 104:4; Heb. 1:7). This hymn also identifies St. Michael as the first among all the heavenly hosts, their chief commander—though he is chief in "devoted obedience" to God, fulfilling God's will, as the previous hymn notes. For this reason, of all the angels, St. Michael appears most often in iconography.

What Are the Angels?

The Scriptures and divine services never undertake to define angels, though we can glean a number of traits from these texts. The Church Fathers take up the task of defining and drawing out theological insight from the texts.[15] A concise, standard source for patristic comment on angels is in Book II of *An Exact Exposition of the Orthodox Faith*, by St. John of Damascus:[16]

> [God] is the maker and creator of angels, bringing them out of non-being into being, having created them after his own image as an incorporeal nature, like some spirit or immaterial fire, as the divine David says, "who makes his angels spirits and his ministers a fiery flame," describing their lightness, ardor, warmth, extreme sharpness,

---

15 Orthodox Christians use the terms *Church Fathers, Holy Fathers,* or simply *the Fathers* to refer to authoritative and sainted teachers in the Church's Tradition, especially from the first millennium of Church history but including Fathers even up to recent years. They are especially respected for their biblical interpretation.

16 Saint John of Damascus was an eighth-century monastic, theologian, and hymnographer who lived in both Damascus and at Mar Sabbas Monastery in Palestine. His *Fount of Knowledge,* of which the *Exact Exposition* is a part, is a reliable summary of the patristic tradition up to the eighth century. In this section, I am quoting from various portions of ch. 3, book II of the *Exact Exposition,* though not always in the order they appear, from the Norman Russell translation in *On the Orthodox Faith: Vol. 3 of the Fount of Knowledge* (Yonkers, NY: St. Vladimir's Seminary Press, 2022), 90–115.

> and acuity with regard to their longing for God and ministry to him and their sublimity and deliverance from all material thought.

We have seen this "fiery" language before, and St. John pairs it with "lightness" because the angels are sublime, or, in another translation "borne to the regions above."[17] This language associates the angels with the heavens, the sublime region above the earth. We might find it surprising, however, that St. John says the angels are created by God "after his own image." Doesn't that language belong only to humanity?

In the Orthodox Tradition, to be according to someone's "image" is to resemble him or her in some way, but it is more about doing his or her works. So both humans and the angels are created to be "imagers" of God, doing His works. This connection between doing someone's works and being in his or her image is expressed particularly in the father–son relationship, especially in Christ, the image of the invisible God (Col. 1:15). For this reason, Jesus tells the Judean leaders in John 8 that their father is not Abraham but rather the devil, whose works they do (John 8:39, 44).

Perhaps the most intriguing question regarding angels is whether they have bodies. In Orthodox liturgical texts, we often refer to them as "bodiless." So the short answer would seem to be no. Saint John starts out saying that but then gets more precise:

> An angel is therefore a substance that is intellectual [lit. *noetic*],[18] always moving, possessing free will, incorporeal, ministering to God, whose nature has by grace received immortality, and the form and determining of whose essence only the Creator knows. An angel is

---

17 Saint John of Damascus, *An Exposition of the Orthodox Faith*, bk. II, ch. 3, in *Nicene and Post-Nicene Fathers*, trans. S. D. F. Salmond, eds. Philip Schaff and Henry Wace, vol. 9 (Peabody, MA: Hendrickson Publishers 1999), 19.

18 The *nous* is a spiritual faculty that receives thoughts. *Noetic* is the adjective.

> said to be incorporeal and immaterial in relation to us. For everything in comparison with God, who alone is incomparable, is dense and material, for only the divine is truly immaterial and incorporeal.

Saint John says two things about angelic bodies here. First, he says that angels do not have bodies—they are "incorporeal and immaterial." Yet he also says that compared with God, they are "dense and material" because God alone is truly without materiality (except, of course, in the incarnate Jesus Christ). He elaborates on this in another passage in this same text:

> They are circumscribed, for when they are in heaven, they are not on earth, and when they are sent to the earth by God, they do not remain in heaven. They are not confined by walls and doors, locks and seals, for they are not limited. I say not limited, because they do not appear to the worthy, to those to whom God wills them to appear, as they really are, but in a different form, in such a way that those who behold them can see them. "For properly speaking, only the uncreated is unlimited by nature, for every created thing is limited by God who created it."[19]

He also writes:

> Being intellects [*noes*], they are also in intellectual [*noetic*] places, since they are not circumscribed corporeally (for they do not have by nature a bodily form, nor are they extended three-dimensionally), but they are present and active intellectually [*noetically*] where they are assigned to be and cannot be present and active in two different places simultaneously.

---

19 Saint John is quoting here from a text called *Doctrina Patrum*, a late seventh-century anthology of patristic texts on the Incarnation of Christ.

It is not therefore a contradiction that Orthodox Tradition often calls the angels "bodiless," but we should understand *bodiless* to be in comparison to human beings. In comparison to God, they are embodied. While we do not understand what angelic bodies are or how they work, nor can we see them as they truly are, angels nevertheless have form, limitation, and location, which are known to God.

Saint John goes on to speak of free will with regards to angels:

> An angel, then, is a rational nature possessing intellect and free will that is mutable or changeable with regard to the will of choice. For everything created is also mutable, only that which is uncreated being immutable, and everything rational possesses free will. Therefore as rational and intellectual [*noetic*], the angelic nature possesses free will, but as created it is mutable, since it has the power to choose and either abide in the good and make progress in it or take a turn for the worse.

Let's unpack this. First, angels have free will like humans do—they can choose whether to do good or evil. Saint John says that their changeability comes from being creations, because only the uncreated God is truly unchangeable. Further, because angels are rational, they have free will, the ability to choose to do good or evil.

Next, St. John anticipates a question that might occur to his readers: Why don't fallen angels choose to do good? After all, human beings, who are also fallen, can choose to repent and do good, so why not demons? Is there no hope for them? Saint John writes: "An angel is incapable of repentance because it is incorporeal, for a human being has the possibility of repentance on account of the weakness of the body." By nature, angels cannot repent because they do not have the weakness of mortality that humans do. He does not explain how this works, so we will have to discuss this a bit ourselves to try to understand it.

First, we should notice that choosing good in itself does not seem to constitute repentance for St. John. Rather, one must be capable of repentance, meaning that a person must have the ability to change in this way. Repentance is an existential change that helps one become more like God, not a mere decision to do a good thing. Angels by nature are not capable of that kind of change. From one angle, their inability to repent is because angels do not experience time, *chronos* (linear time), in the way that we humans experience it—time in motion. Rather they exist in *aionos* ("the ages"), which the Church Fathers identify as motion without time. God, however, exists in *adionikos*—timeless, eternal existence. Repentance requires *chronos*.[20]

Humanity is capable of repentance not only because of how we live in time but primarily because of the mortality God grants in Genesis 3:21–23, the "garments of skin" with which He clothes them. We don't know exactly how this works, but there is something about having mortal bodies that makes repentance possible. God gives this gift of repentance to humanity but not to fallen angels—He does not help them in this way (Heb. 2:16). We don't know why. But will yet-unfallen angels fall in the future? Could we, for instance, lose our guardian angels to evil? Saint John says that can't happen anymore: "They are reluctant to move towards evil but are not immovable, only now they are also immovable, not by nature but by grace and their devotion to the only good."

So no more angels will fall because God keeps them from doing so by His grace. An angel who has already fallen is fallen forever because of his immortality, which God sustains in both the fallen and unfallen angels: "An angel is immortal not by nature but by grace, for everything that has a beginning naturally has an end. Only God exists eternally or rather, he is beyond eternity, for he who is the creator of

20 For a thorough examination of time in the Church Fathers, see George Mantzaridis's *Time and Man* (Waymart, PA: St. Tikhon's Monastery Press, 2014).

time is not subject to time but transcends it." This comment about the sustenance God gives to angels is put within the context of eternality and time. Angels experience time in some way because they are created and therefore changeable, but God is not under its dominion, being above it.

Further, their immortality means they "do not need marriage," that is, they do not reproduce, which is the way mortal beings perpetuate their kind. Therefore, although we typically refer to angels with masculine gender pronouns, they are not gendered at all, since they cannot by nature reproduce. So if they cannot reproduce, are they all of one "species" or of many different, unique ones? We don't really know:

> Whether they are equal or differ from each other with regard to essence we do not know. Only God who created them and who knows all things has knowledge of this. [But we do know that] they differ from each other in their illumination and standing, either possessing their standing in proportion to their illumination, or sharing in illumination in proportion to their standing, and they illuminate each other by the superiority of their rank or nature. And it is clear that the superior impart a share of their illumination and knowledge to the inferior.

Saint John uses phenomenological language here, that is, he shows what humans actually can experience. We can observe from the Scriptures and from the experience of the Church that the angels differ from each other in certain ways, including in superiority, but we don't know how that works. God alone knows.

Saint John also describes the angels as "spiritual lights":

> The angels are secondary spiritual [*noetic*] lights that possess their illumination from the first light that has no beginning. They have no

> need of speech or hearing but communicate their own thoughts and intentions to each other without verbal utterance.
>
> All the angels, then, were created by the agency of the Word and were perfected through sanctification by the Holy Spirit in accordance with the dignity and rank of the illumination and grace in which they share.

Their light is derivative, coming from "the first light that has no beginning," that is, God Himself. Not only does this remind us of the association of the angels with the heavenly bodies, but it is also the language of theosis, becoming like God through derivative participation in Him. The sanctification of the Holy Spirit brings them to perfection, with the glory appropriate to their rank. This perfecting experience that the angels have by participating in the uncreated light of God through the power of the Holy Spirit is basically the same dynamic in which human beings also participate in theosis. Because humans share in Christ's human nature, however, our potential is even greater than theirs. We will discuss this more later.

Saint John also says that their communication works through thought, which at least partly explains how humans can communicate with them to ask for their help. They don't need to hear us in the way we need to hear each other.

How do the angels relate to humans? God Himself has set up our relationship to the angels, and He has given them to us for our salvation: "They watch over parts of the earth and are set in charge of nations and places, as appointed by the Creator, and administer our affairs and help us, and being always around God they are necessarily superior to us in accordance with the divine will and command." Here we see angels in the function of guardian patron saints, who tend to us on behalf of God and because of their closeness to Him.

Saint John completes his chapter on the angels by speaking of their creation:

> Now some say that they were brought into being before all creation. For example, Gregory the Theologian says: "First he conceived of the angelic and heavenly powers, and the conception was the accomplished work." But others say that this was after the creation of the first heaven. All hold that it was before the creation of humanity. I, for my part, agree with Gregory the Theologian. For it was necessary that spiritual [*noetic*] substance should be created first, followed by sensible substance, and then humanity from both.

Note that he reports differing views within the Tradition of the Church. Saint Gregory the Theologian says that God made the angels before the visible creation, but others say that God made the heavens first. The Scriptures do not actually say when the angels were made, so there is room for difference of opinion. Saint John says that all agree, however, that God made them before humans, and he also says that he agrees with St. Gregory's view because of how it relates to the creation of humankind, who embody both visible and invisible elements of creation.

Saint John's last word on the angels is a warning ultimately against idolatry, which includes the worship of angels:

> Those who say that the angels are creators of any substance whatsoever are the mouthpiece of their father the devil. For since they are created beings they are not creators. The maker, controller, and sustainer of all things is God, the only uncreated one, who is hymned and glorified in the Father, Son, and Holy Spirit.

The angels are not creators "of any substance." That does not mean they are not capable of exercising what we call "creativity." It means they cannot make things come into being which were not, which is why he says they cannot create substances. For this reason, God, who alone is uncreated, is worthy of our worship.

There is much more we could say about angels, given the many encounters with them that the people of God have experienced over the ages of human history, and also given the extensive traditions of liturgical celebration and invocation of them that the Church has received. What we've covered here, however, should give us a basic framework for understanding who the heavenly hosts are and what their place is in the life of the Christian. We will move on now to those of the hosts who fell away from obedience to God.[21]

Who Are Demons?

What is a demon? In brief, a demon is everything that an angel is, since demons have the nature of angels. They are the same kind of spiritual being, created by God as immortal, incorruptible,[22] and (as compared to us) incorporeal. To be more precise, *demon,* in the ancient context, referred to a lesser spiritual being. In Greek paganism, it was not a negative term. Socrates famously said his wisdom came from a demon, but it becomes a negative term in the biblical tradition. *Demon* in some texts can also refer to demonized human souls. Certain ancient Church Fathers and other Christian texts express the belief in the possibility of human demonization to such an extent that humans can function like fallen angels after death. We will deal with that question in a later chapter.

Everything St. John of Damascus says about angels in terms of their nature can also be said about demons, and it's notable that his

---

21 Father Stephen De Young gives a more detailed account of demons, the devil, the Satan, etc., in ch. 4 of *The Religion of the Apostles,* "Spiritual Powers of Evil and Human Rebellion" (Ancient Faith Publishing, 2021).

22 *Incorruptible* here means that their bodies (however defined) cannot decay or be harmed. It does not mean that they cannot be corrupted in the sense of becoming evil. Likewise, when we refer to the bodies of some saints as *incorrupt,* it means that they are not wholly overtaken by decay, even if there is some degree of decay in them.

chapter on the devil and demons is rather shorter than the one on angels.[23] Because we already therefore have some sense of *what* the demons are, we can move on to *who* they are.

Saint John begins with the devil:

> Of these angelic powers the one who was the protector of the terrestrial order and entrusted by God with the guardianship of the earth was not wicked by nature, but was good, and was made for good, and did not have the slightest trace of evil in him from the Creator.

This point is extremely important. God did not make the demons evil. Indeed, God made nothing evil. A demon is not a different kind of thing from an angel, but rather, it is an angel who has fallen. Saint John says that the devil was originally "the protector of the terrestrial order" and given "the guardianship of the earth," "made for good." In other words, he was an angel, whom God created and gave a task, as He did with all other angels. His intended purpose was to do the good works of God, but he departed from that purpose and fell into evil:

> But he did not maintain within himself the luminosity and honor that the Creator had bestowed on him. By his own free choice he turned from what was in accordance with nature to what was contrary to nature and became puffed up against God who had made him. Wishing to rebel against him, and becoming the first to abandon the good, he fell into evil. . . . An infinite multitude of angels of those subordinate to him detached themselves and followed him and fell with him. Consequently, although of the same nature as angels, they became

23 Chapter 4 of Book II of *An Exact Exposition of the Orthodox Faith*, pages 102–104, from which I'll be quoting in this section. This chapter immediately follows his chapter on angels.

> evil in their will, since they had voluntarily turned away from good towards evil.

So not only was the devil the first to depart into evil, bringing many angels with him, but becoming evil is actually "contrary to [his] nature" as an angel. An angel's nature is to serve God and to do good, so if an angel departs from that way, he is actually fighting not only God but himself. The same is true of humans. That is why there is a darkening within any person who sins. Rebellion against God destroys the one who falls into it.

Saint John also says something important here about the nature of evil: "For evil is nothing other than the privation of good, just as darkness is the privation of light." Evil, therefore, is not a *thing* as such. It is only the distortion or deprivation of something good. God's creation is ordered and full of what is good. Genesis 1 is precisely the story of how God brings order and fullness to creation, giving it structure in Genesis 1:1–10, and then filling up that structure in Genesis 1:11–31. God gives humanity the mission of continuing His work, both to order the earth and to fill it (Gen. 1:28). For this reason, we can think of demons as chaos monsters. To rebel against order and fullness is to embrace chaos and emptiness. It is to try to return to the state of things before God began to shape the earth, when it was formless (chaotic) and void (empty) (Gen. 1:2). When demons attack humans, therefore, they seek to empty them of good and to destroy their shape, both material and spiritual.

The most prominent of all demons is the devil, who is introduced as the serpent in Eden in Genesis 3. What is a talking serpent doing in Eden? He is a seraph, one of the throne guardians—remember that seraphim are traditionally depicted as serpentine. It is therefore from this imagery of a fallen serpentine angel that dragons get associated with evil. That said, dragon imagery never gets completely consigned to evil in the Christian tradition. One can still see dragons depicted on vestments, iconostases, and other holy items used in worship. Clearly, these are images of seraphim.

What Do Demons Do?

If angels are as powerful as the Scriptures and Church Tradition witness to, then demons truly are frightening to consider. Angels are vast cosmic intelligences, immaterial and capable of influencing all the elements of creation. They can appear to humans in almost infinite shapes. What if such a being falls into evil, seeking to deceive us and to push the creation back toward chaos? Saint John gives us assurance:

> They therefore do not have any authority or power over anybody unless they are granted it by the dispensation of God, as in the case of Job, just as is recorded about the swine in the Gospel. When God gives his permission, they have the power to change and transform into whatever illusory form they wish.

So even though they are deceptive shapeshifters in their appearance, God restrains them, and they can do only what He wills—this should give us some peace. Saint John goes on to address what else they are capable of:

> With regard to what belongs to the future, neither the angels nor the demons have knowledge of it. They do, however, foretell it, in the case of God's angels when he reveals it to them and commands them to foretell it. It is thus that what they say comes to pass. The demons also foretell, sometimes by seeing what is still a long way off, and sometimes by guesswork, which means that they are generally wrong. One should not believe them, even if they frequently tell the truth in the manner that we have described. Besides, they know the Scriptures.

Of course, a being of vast cosmic intelligence will have much greater knowledge than human beings, including of the Scriptures. Yet they still are not God, and they do not have infinite power or knowledge. We should therefore not be deceived by knowledge that comes from demons, even if it seems uncannily accurate.

The mission of demons is to try to destroy us, and as we can see from the Scriptures, the origins of evil in humankind lie with demons.[24] Saint John expresses this same truth, that sin comes from demons: "Therefore every evil has been devised by them, along with the unclean passions. And although they have been permitted to tempt humanity, they are not able to force anyone. For it rests with us to accept the temptation or not to accept it." There is hope here, that we can resist demonic power. Humans can choose to accept their temptations or not. Nevertheless, they can do evil. Why does God even allow this to begin with?

Why Does God Let Demons Attack Humans?

At the opening of this chapter, I quote from St. Gregory the Dialogist (also known as St. Gregory the Great). Here it is again with more context:

> For what is the throne of the Lord, unless we understand the Angelic Powers, in whose minds enthroned on high He disposeth all things below? And what is the host of heaven, unless the multitude of ministering Angels is set forth? Why then is it, that the

24 As I detail in *Arise, O God*, the three evils of humankind—death, sin, and domination by dark powers—all come through demonic activity. Respectively, these three arise with the temptation by the serpent in Genesis 3, the overwhelming of Cain and his family with sin in Genesis 4, and the rule of the nations by demons through idolatry following the Babel event in Genesis 11.

> host of heaven is said to stand on His right hand and on His left? For God, Who is in such sort within all things, that He is also without all, is neither bounded on the right hand nor on the left. However, the right hand of God is the elect portion of the Angels, and the left hand of God signifies the reprobate portion of Angels. For not alone do the good serve God by the aid which they render, but likewise the wicked by the trials which they inflict; not only they who lift upward them that are turning back from transgression, but they who press down those who refuse to turn back. Nor because it is called the host of heaven, are we hindered from understanding therein the reprobate portion of the Angels, for whatsoever birds we know to be poised in the air, we call them "the birds of heaven." And it is of these same spirits that Paul saith, Against spiritual wickedness in high places. And describing their head, he says, According to the prince of the power of the air. On the right hand and on the left hand of God, then, stands the Angelic Host, forasmuch as both the will of the elect spirits harmonizes with Divine mercy, and the mind of the reprobate, in serving their own evil ends, obeys the judgment of His strict decrees.[25]

Here St. Gregory addresses the question of why God permits demons to do what they wish to do, "when they serve their own evil ends." He is commenting on 1 Kings 22, when the prophet Micaiah speaks to Ahab, the king of the Northern Kingdom of Israel. The prophet tells how in heaven God spoke to the angels at His right and left (1 Kin. 22:19). God asks who will make sure that Ahab dies in battle, and one spirit says that he will put a "lying spirit" into the mouths of Ahab's prophets, making him think he will be victorious. God sends that spirit out to do what he said (22:21–23).

---

25 Saint Gregory the Dialogist, *Moralia in Job*, 2.38.

Putting a lying spirit in the mouths of prophets is an act of evil, a demonic act, so the spirit who does this is a fallen angel. Yet we see that God restrains him and he can do only what God wills. God permits the spirit to do this evil. Thus, the spirit gets to do what he likes—to bring about death and destruction. Likewise, it is God's will to judge Ahab for his evil, and so Ahab's arrogance in going into battle brings him to that judgment.

So are demons the instruments of the judgment of God? If by *judgment* we mean the ending of wickedness, that is true, but there is also a sense of *judgment* here that is apropos. The purpose of God's justice is to set things right, to put them back into the order that He created. In some cases, this will mean the downfall of the wicked, but God's justice also can involve repentance both for the wicked and for the holy who desire to advance even further in holiness.

Consider how St. Paul saw that the demon who tormented him helped him fight the temptation to feel prideful: "So to keep me from becoming conceited because of the surpassing greatness of the revelations, a thorn was given me in the flesh, a messenger [literally, *angel*] of Satan to harass me, to keep me from becoming conceited" (2 Cor. 12:7). God was not punishing St. Paul for his sins. Rather, God gave him the opportunity to advance in holiness. When God permits demons to attack humans, it is to give them the opportunity for repentance.

I will say one more word here about the demon who inspired Ahab's prophets to speak lies: Ahab of course does not believe what Micaiah says to him. He listens instead to his own prophets and proceeds to his destruction. Yet notice what is happening here. By relating the story of the conversation between God and the angels at His left and right, Micaiah is letting Ahab know about the lying spirit. In other words, Ahab is being given an opportunity to repent. Ahab does not take it, but God in His merciful love for Ahab provides the means of salvation even to that wicked man.

The Fate of Demons

What will happen to demons because of their wickedness? Saint John again gives the answer. After saying that they are the source of all wickedness and impure passions, he tells us what God has in store for them: "Wherefore there has been prepared for the devil and his demons, and those who follow him, fire unquenchable and everlasting punishment" (see Matt. 25:41).

We saw above how demons, by virtue of being incorruptible angels and not having mortal bodies, are incapable of repentance. Their nature is such that they do not even want it. They do not sit in their fallenness, feeling regret and wishing they could just change back into angels if only God would let them. Such feelings are a human reality, and we should not ascribe them to spiritual beings—we do not know what it is like to be an angel or demon. Additionally, the fall into evil is a one-way trip for demons, as St. John goes on to say: "One also needs to know that what death is for human beings, the fall is for angels. For after the fall there is no repentance for them, just as there is no repentance for human beings after death." They cannot and will not repent. Any speculation that they might want to is not warranted and requires imagining them basically to be very powerful humans.

Notice, however, that St. John embeds a warning here for us, too. The unquenchable fire and everlasting punishment reserved for the devil and his demons also is appointed for "those who follow them," that is, for unrepentant humans. Likewise, while after a fall angels cannot repent, after death humans cannot repent. Why? Both are in states in which they lack a mortal, corruptible body, which is necessary for repentance, as well as the *aionos* ("the ages") into which humans move after death.

According to Orthodox Tradition, the possibility exists for unrepentant humans to be saved after death by virtue of the repentance of the living on their behalf—primarily, the prayers that we offer to

God for His mercy upon them. No one should count on this mercy, however. This life we have now is for our repentance. The fate of the demonic powers should not be something we become overly curious about, but God offers us knowledge of it in limited form for the same reason he gives us everything else—for our own repentance.

Having looked at angels and demons in general in the Scriptures and elsewhere in Orthodox Tradition, we will now turn to some particular monstrous entities we find in the Bible.

CHAPTER 3

Biblical Monsters

Can you draw out Leviathan with a fishhook / or press down his tongue with a cord? / Can you put a rope in his nose / or pierce his jaw with a hook? Will he make many pleas to you? / Will he speak to you soft words? / Will he make a covenant with you / to take him for your servant forever? / Will you play with him as with a bird, / or will you put him on a leash for your girls? / Will traders bargain over him? / Will they divide him up among the merchants? / Can you fill his skin with harpoons / or his head with fishing spears?

—Job 41:1–7

And the heart itself is but a little vessel, and yet there are found dragons and lions and venomous beasts and all the treasures of evil. And there are rough, uneven ways and chasms. But likewise, God, the angels, life, and the Kingdom are found there, and light and the apostles and the heavenly cities and the good treasure—there are all things found.

—St. Makarios the Great[1]

1 Saint Makarios the Great, *The Fifty Spiritual Homilies* 43:7, trans. A. J. Mason (Florence, AZ: SAGOM Press, 2020), 335.

We began this book by saying that there are dragons in the Bible. There are also dragons in other early Christian texts. Before we discuss why these creatures are there, let's have a look at a number of the dragon references and stories, as well as some other monsters we find in the Scriptures. Since these monsters are demonic in character, we do not need to spend time asking *what* they are. What is more interesting, in any event, is *who* they are—that is, what are their actual characters in the accounts we have of them?

Leviathan

The greatest of all dragons in Christian tradition is a massive, primordial sea serpent the Scripture refers to as *Leviathan* (Job 3:8, 41:1; Ps. 74:14, 104:26; Is. 27:1) and also as *Rahab* or *Rahav* (Job 9:13, 26:12; Ps. 89:10; Is. 30:7, 51:9. This creature should not be confused with the woman Rahab of Jericho in the Book of Joshua, though it is the same name). The association of a serpentine image with a demonic force begins in the Scriptures with Genesis 3, with the serpent tempting the first humans into sin. From there the image expands and grows considerably in size until we get Leviathan, an immense sea dragon associated with primal forces of chaos.

As we will discuss in the next chapter, the sea is traditionally associated with chaos and death. Even in our more technologically advanced era, the raging of the sea is impossible for human beings to master. So while our period tends to look at the power of the sea as mindless, without any kind of will driving it, pre-modern people saw it as moved by unseen spiritual forces—much like they saw the rest of creation. Especially because the force of the sea was destructive, they tended to look upon its animating spirit as demonic rather than benevolent. Thus, the tradition of the Bible and many other ancient religions viewed the seas as moved by the thrashing of a great underwater dragon.

This sea dragon was not usually depicted like the dragons we see in movies and fantasy novels in our time, with four legs and large wings, roughly of similar body shape to land animals who walk on four legs. Rather, it was more like a great snake, perhaps with small legs or wings, though it did not need them since it moved by swimming rather than walking or flying.

Leviathan's most thorough biblical description comes in Job 41, in which God humbles Job for his impudence in challenging Him, asking if Job is able to defeat or tame Leviathan by drawing him up with a fishhook, tying up his nose and jaw, etc. (Job 41:1–2 and following). This dragon is not only fierce beyond any man's power (41:10) but also mighty in strength (41:12), with terrifying teeth (41:14), powerfully armored (41:15–17), with sneezes like lightning (41:18), and breathing fire (41:19–21). No human being can defeat him, no matter how heroic, and he is so exalted in his haughtiness that he is "king over all the sons of pride" (41:34).

This dragon is beyond most of the dragons one sees in other literature. Leviathan is a force of demonic chaos that only God can defeat. God is the one "ready to rouse up Leviathan" (Job 3:8). God will crush "the heads of Leviathan" and feed him to "the creatures of the wilderness" (Ps. 74:14). This eschatological battle will be the redemption of Israel: "In that day the Lord with his hard and great and strong sword will punish Leviathan the fleeing serpent, Leviathan the twisting serpent, and he will slay the dragon that is in the sea" (Is. 27:1).

This draconic image is not only eschatological but also figures into Israel's origin story. Isaiah 51 credits God as the one "who cut Rahab in pieces, / who pierced the dragon" (51:9), which is put in the context of the drying up of the sea so that the redeemed may pass over, a reference to the Exodus of Israel from Egypt (51:10). At the same time, of course, Israel's origin in the Exodus is one of the images for the eschatological redemption of the Church.

Narratively speaking, the association of the defeat of Leviathan with the Exodus in Isaiah 51 almost forms a kind of *ouroboros* in which the serpent is present and being defeated at both the beginning and the end of time. Some medieval texts liken Leviathan to the ouroboros, so we might wonder whether the biblical Leviathan is the same kind of being. But what is an ouroboros? An ouroboros is an ancient circular symbol of a serpentine figure swallowing its own tail. Some contexts have interpreted it as representing an endless cycle of life and/or death, as seen, for instance, in Vedic (Hindu) texts, which sometimes liken rituals to the tail-eating serpent, illustrating the cyclic view of time in that religious tradition. Some mythology also deploys the circular serpent to refer to an ancient oceanic serpent that holds the world together. In Norse mythology, for instance, Jörmungandr (*Miðgarðsormr,* the Midgard serpent) fulfills this role, and serpents eating their tails are found in art not only in Indo-European traditions but in Egypt and China.

So is Leviathan really an ouroboros? While there are some similarities, the dissimilarities are significant. In the Scriptures, Leviathan does not hold the world together. God is the one who has put the world in place so that it cannot be moved (Ps. 93:1). Further, though we certainly might say this about demonic beings, the Bible never depicts Leviathan as devouring itself. Indeed, Leviathan will get devoured, but it is God's people who will finally eat Leviathan after God cuts him into pieces, part of the nourishment they will receive as God renews the whole creation (Ps. 74:12–17).

Psalm 74 associates Leviathan with the seas, but not only with the sea in general. Verse 12 says that God divides "the sea" by His might. The Hebrew word there for "sea" is *Yam,* which is the name of the Canaanite god of the sea.[2] Leviathan's association with Yam is not something

2 Yam is the most high god of Canaanite mythology until Baal defeats him and puts his father El on the throne.

the Bible invents but rather references. In Canaanite mythology (attested in the Ugaritic *Baal Cycle*), Leviathan (*Litanu* or *Lotan*) is the primary sea serpent Yam deploys to exercise his power.[3] By using the name *Leviathan* and associating him with the sea god Yam, the Bible directly references the great mythic sea serpent known throughout the ancient Near East. In Canaanite mythology, Baal defeats Leviathan, but in the Bible, it is God who defeats Leviathan (and Baal, too, as we will see later).

Thus, when God "divides" Yam, breaks the heads of sea monsters (Ps. 74:13), and crushes the heads of Leviathan (74:14), the initial impression is of God overcoming the powers of the high gods of the Canaanites. From what we have seen about the ubiquity of serpentine images in the world's pagan religious traditions, however, we can see that ultimately God's defeat of Leviathan is about the defeat of the demonic powers that encircle and animate evil in the world, regardless of which religious tradition represents them. It is not only about the Canaanite serpentine chaos monsters, but about all of them.

The Bible's depiction of God's relationship to Leviathan is not only about the latter's defeat by His might, however. If we left the imagery there, we might conclude that God and the ancient chaos serpent are perhaps rivals, and God comes out on top. That is basically how Baal relates to Leviathan. Thor relates similarly to Jörmungandr, though at the eschatological Norse Ragnarok, they are so evenly matched that they kill each other. God also relates to Leviathan, but in another way.

At Vespers every day in the Orthodox Church, the faithful hear Psalm 104. In this psalm's depiction of God's ordering of the

3 Job mentions Leviathan and Rahab separately, apparently as two different serpentine powers of Yam rather than two names for the same power. The *Baal Cycle* also mentions a serpent called Tannin who serves Yam, and in the Old Testament, *tanninim* are chaotic sea serpents. Israel uses both *Rahab* and *Tannin* after the Exodus to refer to Egypt.

world, Leviathan is mentioned as being formed to "play" in the seas (104:26). Here Leviathan seems almost like God's pet, a sea creature who is utterly subservient to God and under His control. Leviathan is a chaos monster, though, so how does this make sense? Genesis 1 initially describes Creation as God bringing order to chaos (1:1–10). We also see how chaos is always just outside the door in a sense, as when God removes His protection and the great Flood comes (Gen. 7:11). We can understand God's proper ordering of the world, therefore, not only as the defeat of demonic powers but also as holding the powers of chaos in check. Leviathan thus participates in the dynamic we saw in the previous chapter, in which demonic powers do what they wish, but God's restraining hand makes them ultimately serve His will. And as we saw above, Leviathan's ultimate fate is to nourish the renewed creation at the end of time.

These mythic-level understandings of Leviathan are significant for us, as they demonstrate one of the ways we can understand how God deals with demonic powers. That said, there is a particular application of the spirit of Leviathan and God's defeat of it that we can perhaps immediately comprehend, and that has to do with how Leviathan manifests not just in mythological texts but in direct, everyday human experience.

In Daniel 7, the prophet's vision includes beasts that rise up out of the sea, monstrous and bizarre in appearance, which hold dominion over the earth (7:3–8). The prophet says that these sea monsters represent kingdoms of the earth (7:17). The horrors that these demonic spirits unleash are chaotic and destructive, and this depiction of oceanic chaos demons is another way of representing the spirit of Leviathan. The fourth beast in particular is of note, "different from all the rest, exceedingly terrifying, with its teeth of iron and claws of bronze, and which devoured and broke in pieces and stamped what was left with its feet" (7:19). God Himself gives the interpretation: "As for the fourth beast, there shall be a fourth kingdom on earth, / which shall be different from all the kingdoms, / and it shall devour the whole earth, / and trample it down, and break it to pieces" (7:23). This kingdom is an imperial kingdom, not content merely to exercise dominion within its own sphere but wishing to eat up the whole earth, to bring chaos and destruction everywhere, and even to make war on the saints (7:21).[4]

This is how empire works. The Roman historian Tacitus, in his *Agricola*, memorably quotes Calgacus, a Celtic enemy of Rome, who says of the Romans:

> These plunderers of the world, after exhausting the land by their devastations, are rifling the ocean: stimulated by avarice, if their enemy be rich; by ambition, if poor; unsatiated by the East and by the West: the only people who behold wealth and indigence with equal avidity. To ravage, to slaughter, to usurp under false titles, they call empire; and where they make a desert, they call it peace.[5]

Humans in every age have seen what imperial ambition does, making deserts that are thereby called "peace." This imperial drive is the spirit of Leviathan, unleashing chaos until everything has been so destroyed that there is submission through devastation.

What makes empires distinct? It is not that they are tribes and nations but rather that they seek to impose their rule and way of thinking and life upon others who already belong to some other people. Peoples have a shared way of life that they don't project afar, but empires are totalizing and demand that everyone live and think in

---

4 Revelation 13:1–10 "remixes" Daniel 7, with a sea beast rising out of the water that is also closely associated with a dragon that makes war on the saints. As in Daniel 7, the saints win and receive dominion from God.

5 Tacitus, *The Agricola* (Urbana, IL: Project Gutenberg, 2013), sec. 30, https://www.gutenberg.org/files/7524/7524-h/7524-h.htm.

one uniform way. Isn't the gospel therefore a kind of empire? No, it is not. Why? The gospel converts everyone to Christ, within which there are many ways of thinking and living, and the gospel creates local communities that have a shared way. The gospel, in other words, through love builds communities that are varied and distinct. It does not conquer through empire. Empire is evangelism through the sword, which is not evangelism at all but really its opposite.

What about on the individual level? Most of us, of course, are not emperors. Though not emperors, we would do well not to admire them, at least not for their imperial achievements. Most of us have unleashed chaos, however, bringing destruction to those around us in our desire to have things our own way, to devour and be filled at any cost.

We also sometimes worship power, whether that worship is aimed at actual empires or other powerful figures, giving them what is due to God alone. We can therefore recognize the animating spirit of Leviathan not only in the way that some nations try to swallow up and control others, but also in the way that we try to do that ourselves and the way that we perpetuate it through giving ourselves over to power.

Behemoth

Another demonic figure from the Bible, related to Leviathan and who in some sense is his counterpart, is Behemoth. *Behemoth* comes from the singular *behema,* which means "cow." The form *behemoth* is a plural generally meaning "cows," but when Hebrew biblical texts refer to this demonic force, they treat it as a singular. The plural with this application is meant to indicate intensity. Thus, *Behemoth* means "beast of beasts." Behemoth is *The* Beast, the most beastly of all beasts. In the Scripture, Behemoth is essentially a giant, powerful bull.

Bulls are among the most ancient and pervasive of all images from pagan idolatry. We recall not only the golden calves the Israelites worshiped at various points when they went astray from God, but also that bulls are found in almost every pagan mythology. In Greek mythology, for instance, Zeus transforms himself into a bull in order to abduct and seduce a maiden named Europa.[6] Egyptians worshiped a bull deity named Apis (possibly the origin of the Israelites' calves), the Sumerian Marduk was associated with bulls, and so was the Mesopotamian storm god Hadad. Çatalhöyük in Turkey, one of the most ancient archaeological sites, includes bull images in the dwellings of its residents. In Baal worship, the god in his guise as the lord of death was presented as a bull to represent his power and virility, and he is depicted wearing a horned helmet.[7] Bulls in cultic contexts historically appear nearly everywhere in the world, from cave paintings to statues to ritual bathing in bulls' blood.

The pagans associated the bull with power, virility, and the dominion of death. From the biblical point of view, if Leviathan is the ultimate demon of chaos, then Behemoth is the ultimate demon of tyranny. Since worship of bulls is so ubiquitous in ancient paganism, we might wonder at this identification of Behemoth with tyranny—why worship a tyrant? We will discuss in a later chapter what worship is and how it works, but for now, we will say that people worship tyrants for two reasons—to placate them so that they are less dangerous and to identify with them and receive some of their power.

In the Scriptures, Behemoth first appears in Job 40, which immediately precedes the passage describing Leviathan:

> Behold, Behemoth, / which I made as I made you. / He eats grass like an ox. / Behold, his strength is in his loins, / and his power in the muscles of his belly / He makes his tail stiff like a cedar; / the sinews

6 It is generally held that Europe is named for her. In the myth, Zeus abducts and rapes her, and she gives birth to Minos, king of Crete. In some versions, she also gives birth to the minotaur, who is half-bull and half-human.

7 Baal's bovine hypostasis was even worshiped with rituals involving bestiality.

> of his thighs are knit together. / His bones are tubes of bronze, / his limbs like bars of iron.
>
> He is the first of the works of God; / let him who made him bring near his sword! / For the mountains yield food for him / where all the wild beasts play. / Under the lotus plants he lies, / in the shelter of the reeds and in the marsh. / For his shade the lotus trees cover him; / the willows of the brook surround him. / Behold, if the river is turbulent he is not frightened; / he is confident though Jordan rushes against his mouth. / Can one take him by his eyes, / or pierce his nose with a snare? (Job 40:15–24)

Here, God describes Behemoth, and paired with Leviathan in the next chapter, the image is of two primal spiritual forces, one in the sea and the other on the land. Four Ezra says that God made them on the fifth day of creation, along with the other aquatic and terrestrial creatures.[8] They are fallen, however, as the whole earth is fallen, which is why Leviathan is chaos unleashed and Behemoth is dominion turned to tyranny. One might liken Leviathan to toxic femininity and Behemoth to toxic masculinity—they are fallen, inflated, destructive distortions of these two sides of creation.[9]

Isaiah 30:6–7 mentions Behemoth again, where with Leviathan (as Rahab) he is associated with Egypt. If in pursuing other nations Egypt externally wields the imperial force of Leviathan, Egypt is internally tyrannical within its own lands as Behemoth. The sea dragon lashes out, while the great bull stampedes within. We see this same kind of language with the "beast rising out of the earth" in Revelation 13:11–18. The passage describes the beast's image and mark as dominating

---

8 4 Ezra 6:49–52. Four Ezra, also called 2 Esdras, is in the Bible of the Russian Orthodox Church.

9 This assignment as male and female in this way is made in the extra-biblical Jewish text 1 Enoch 60:7–9.

all of humankind, even in the buying and selling of goods. In the end, however, God will defeat both of these beasts who make war upon the saints; He will take away their power and give rulership to the saints whom the beasts had attacked (Rev. 5:10, 20:4–6, 22:5).

As we saw earlier with Leviathan, God will eventually cut up Behemoth and give the beast as food to His people, part of a great, eschatological, sacrificial feast He prepares (Ez. 39:17–20). The Ezekiel reference is not explicit, but other texts from Jewish and Christian tradition refer to the great feasting on Leviathan and Behemoth together.[10] What does this mean, that at the end of the world, God will feed Leviathan and Behemoth to the Church? On the one hand, it is a reversal of how things are in this world now, where demons devour human beings. The devil, for instance, is "like a roaring lion, seeking someone to devour" (1 Pet. 5:8). But there is something more here.

The end of time is about God bringing justice—order and vindication—to a chaotic, oppressive world. These forces of destruction and tyranny have been part of human experience throughout all time. But God did not design the things He has made to be harmful to us. Rather, this creation was supposed to be nourishing and beneficial to us. Therefore, when the Scriptures and other traditional texts depict Leviathan and Behemoth as being defeated and turned into food, it is an indication that creation is being returned to its proper Edenic state. In Eden, all things were for the benefit of Adam and Eve, and in the end of time, God will again place humanity in an Edenic context. What has been used for evil will be turned to good.

10 4 Ezra 6:49–52; 2 Baruch 29:4; Apocalypse of Abraham 21:4.

Lilith

There is one more biblical monster I wanted to mention, which is not really directly connected to these beasts we've been discussing. But because this creature is so well-known and indeed mentioned in the Bible, it seems wise to include it. Also, this demonic being will serve as a paradigmatic stand-in for lesser demons we may meet. This demon is called Lilith.

If you have heard of Lilith, you might have heard it said that she was Adam's first wife. Of course, you can search the whole Bible in vain and find no reference to Adam having any wife other than Eve; it is certainly not in Genesis. Those who read the Scriptures with the hermeneutic of suspicion and are inclined to doubt the Scriptures' integrity might see the absence of Lilith from the Genesis story as an indication of tampering with the biblical text—the "truth" about Adam's first wife has been suppressed. There is no actual evidence to support this idea, however. It is pure conjecture.

So where does this idea come from? The earliest known reference to Lilith as Adam's first wife is in the anonymous *Alphabet of Sirach*, which was written from within a Muslim country sometime between AD 700 and 1000, some 3,000 years after the traditional dating of the composition of Genesis around 2000 BC. No prior extant Jewish or Christian literature references its Lilith story. Some modern Jews consider the *Alphabet* to be anti-Jewish literature. The *Alphabet* is a compilation of two lists of proverbs, one in Jewish Babylonian Aramaic and the other in medieval Hebrew, followed by commentary. A number of them can be traced to earlier Jewish sources. It is called an "alphabet" because the lists are arranged as acrostics, each one beginning with one of the twenty-two letters of the Hebrew alphabet.

In the second list, the proverbs are used primarily as introductions to a series of fables, and the Lilith tale appears in one of these stories.

In the tale, after God makes Lilith for Adam out of the same clay as Adam (rather than out of his side as with Eve), the two begin to argue over how they will reproduce.[11] When they reach an impasse, Lilith speaks the name of God and flies up into the air. Adam prays to God to bring Lilith back to him, and God sends three angels after her to offer an ultimatum—return, or one hundred of her children will die every day. She refuses to return, so they threaten her with death. Lilith tells them to leave her alone and declares that she will have dominion over male infants for eight days and females for twenty days, that the true purpose of her creation is to cause sickness to infants. She promises to leave them alone, however, if she sees the angels or their names on amulets. Thus, the tale says, one hundred demons (Lilith's "children") die every day, and pious Jews write the names of angels on the amulets of young children so that Lilith will spare them.

In the medieval period, this depiction of Lilith gets merged with stories about Asmodeus, king of demons, whom the rabbinic Jewish Talmud mentions. She thus is queen of the demons, endlessly procreating demons with Asmodeus. Assuming that it was written by a pious Jew and not as anti-Jewish satire, the purpose of including the story appears ultimately to be the recommendation to ward off the demon Lilith by the invocation of angels, including through talismanic amulets.

This story lived in relative obscurity until the seventeenth-century German scholar Johannes Buxtorf popularized it in his *Lexicon Talmudicum*. From there we get the modern recognition of the name *Lilith* as the first wife of Adam, and the absence of this story from the biblical text is sometimes taken as evidence of a conspiracy to edit out embarrassing bits from the Bible.

---

11 If you are interested in more details, you can find the full account of the story by searching online.

So what's the true story of Lilith? It turns out that the medieval legends and folktales are based on something in Scripture, but it has nothing to do with Adam. In Isaiah 34:14, we read: "And wild animals shall meet with hyenas; / the wild goat shall cry to his fellow; / indeed, there the night bird [Heb. *lilith*] settles / and finds for herself a resting place." In this passage, Edom, the desolated place it speaks of, has experienced the judgment of God. Verse 13 calls Edom a "habitation of dragons [Heb. *tannin*]," and various translations (in the ESV quoted above, "hyenas" and "wild goats") speak of other creatures, along with the *tannin* and *lilith,* as demons, goat-demons, monsters, etc. So we get the sense of a collection of demonic creatures haunting the place, including something called *lilith*.

The Hebrew *lilith* in that verse gets translated into English in a lot of ways: besides "night bird" (ESV), we also get "screech owl" (KJV), "night creature(s)" (NKJV, NIV), "night monster" (NASB 1977/1995), "nocturnal animals" (NET), etc. Probably the oddest versions are in translations that come via the Greek Old Testament, translating *onokentauroi,* where you get the very literal "donkey-centaurs" (NETS, OSB) and "satyrs" (Brenton).

The Hebrew *lilith* comes from the Akkadian loanword *lilitu,* itself borrowed from Sumerian *lil.*[12] This term shows up in the Sumerian text *Gilgamesh, Enkidu, and the Netherworld,* in which the goddess Inanna finds a serpentine demon named *ki-sikil-lil-lu* (note the *lil* there) curled around the roots of a tree she had planted. In Akkadian texts, there are demons named *lilu, lilitu,* and *wardat lili,* which are related to stormy winds. This association with the winds is likely where we get the idea that *lilith* has something to do with the air and why several translations of Isaiah 34:14 render the word as different birds.

12 This linguistic and mythological analysis largely comes from the *Dictionary of Deities and Demons in the Bible,* eds. Karel van der Toorn, Bob Becking, and Pieter W. van der Hoorst (Boston: Brill, 1999,) 520–521.

Akkadian texts, including *lilitu* and *wardat lili,* describe the demons as young women who have no husbands wandering about. They thus travel around trying to ensnare men sexually, including by entering the homes of men through open windows. The texts describe their sexuality as being of a different kind than that between men and women, and they are infertile and give poisonous milk to any babies they encounter. Their character is similar to the Babylonian Lamashtu, which threatens women and their new babies and tries to steal infants. Lilith and Lamashtu over time became assimilated with each other, regarded as different names for the same demonic being.

Lilith does show up in the Jewish Talmud as a demon with long hair and wings, and it includes a warning against men sleeping alone in a house, lest Lilith seduce them. This demonic figure is thus essentially a succubus. We have already seen the medieval legend from the *Alphabet of Sirach* about Lilith being Adam's first wife, but in some Christian legends from the period she is the grandmother of the devil, a source of witchcraft, and the chief of all witches.

So what is going on with the Greek versions, and why "donkey-centaurs"? *Onokentauros* (literally "donkey-centaur") comes from one Greek translation, usually referred to as the Septuagint (LXX). Aside from being a generally weird, monstrous creature, "donkey-centaur" is not an obvious translation of the Semitic and Sumerian terms. It is plausible, however, when considering that the related Babylonian figure Lamashtu is sometimes depicted as a person standing on a donkey.

Other ancient Greek translations treat the Hebrew *lilith* differently. Aquila has *lilith* transliterated into Greek characters, while Symmachus uses the Greek demon name *Lamia.* In Greek mythology, Lamia is a woman raped by Zeus, whom the goddess Hera curses to become a child-eating, serpentine monster who can never sleep. Saint Jerome thus refers in his commentary to "Lamia, who is called

Lilith," also identifying her with the Greek Furies, and so *Lamia* gets into his Latin Vulgate translation.[13]

What are we to make of this Lilith material and of demons like her? In the general sense, we see that there are demonic forces smaller than creatures like Leviathan and Behemoth but also not identified as being the devil. The world has many demons that would ensnare humanity and lead us into sin. More specifically with this creature, Lilith is a demon not so much of infertility but of anti-fertility. In the first place, Lilith is about the destruction of babies—she steals human infants, kills them, or makes them sick. Second, Lilith is also about the propagation of the demonic—with Asmodeus, she spawns little demons. But Lilith is also about the destruction of fertility itself—men are given over to sexual desire that is antithetical to the production of offspring.

We get the sense that Lilith haunts destroyed places—places where destruction, barrenness, and darkness fill what once had life. This desolation is the result of sexuality out of control, turned against humanity. Even the legend of Lilith as Adam's first wife is itself about failed reproduction, about desire for fruitfulness, which then turns to spite and violence. Even the whimsical notion that Lilith is the devil's grandmother is paired with witchcraft, the compulsion to control through manipulation. It is about selfish desire without responsibility.

We can imagine numerous ways in which the demonic force of Lilith is felt especially in our own day, when so much has turned against the blessing—and obedience, per God's initial command to Adam and Eve (Gen. 1:28)—of human fertility. Sexuality in our time has become deeply distorted, and it is directed more and more toward sterility. While Leviathan and Behemoth animate conquest

---

13 Jerome, *Commentarii in Isaiam* 5.13, in Migne, *Patrologia Latina*, XXIV, col. 159.

and tyranny, especially at the societal level, Lilith affects human life at a very personal level, with broad effects in a community, and the spirit that influences humanity in this way is notable for its viciousness and insatiability, much like an angry, demonic succubus.

Why Do Dragons Even Exist?

Author and scholar J. R. R. Tolkien, when giving a 1938 lecture to schoolchildren at a museum, said this about the legends of dragons: "For the most remarkable thing about the great dragons of legend is that their legends mostly tell of their overthrow."[14] Curiously, the lecture began with the professor showing the children a series of slides of dinosaurs. So does Tolkien mean that dragons are just dinosaurs?

Let's consider another illustration about dragons and dinosaurs. I once had a conversation with icon-carver and cultural commentator Jonathan Pageau about dragons, and he said that dragons—chaos monsters that "almost exist"—and dinosaurs are related to each other narratively, but they each relate to humans differently. One thing in particular he went on to say lodged in my memory: "Dragons exist way more than dinosaurs!"[15] What could he have meant by that?

Are dragons just dinosaurs found in stories? What do Tolkien and Pageau's comments have in common? In both cases, they put dragons into relationship with human beings in terms of their place in stories. In Pageau's comments, dragons are chaos monsters that "almost exist," just on the edge of our experience, crossing boundaries and

---

14 From "Dragons" in *J.R.R. Tolkien, The Hobbit, 1937–2017: A Commemorative Booklet Celebrating the 80th Anniversary*, in *The Hobbit: Facsimile Gift Set*, eds. Christina Scull and Wayne G. Hammond (London: HarperCollins, 2018), 49–50.

15 Andrew Stephen Damick, "In Full Fire: Pageau and the Dragons," August 25, 2020, in *Amon Sûl*, podcast, https://www.ancientfaith.com/podcasts/amonsul/028_in_full_fire_pageau_and_the_dragons.

representing chaos as an untameable force. For Tolkien, dragons exist in legendary stories so that they can be overthrown. They are the final test of the hero. Dragons do not therefore have an independent existence from humans but only a phenomenological one. That is, dragons exist as a part of human experience, as described not only in stories and legends but also in canonical Scripture. That does not make them unreal, because the experience of them is real. The same holds true of specific demonic entities such as Leviathan, Behemoth, or Lilith. And as Christians, we know that the demonic is real, even if we cannot measure it empirically.

For this reason, dragons are indeed "more real" than dinosaurs because while we can think about dinosaurs by seeing pictures in books, reading stories about dinosaurs, or (at most) seeing taxidermic recreations in museums, these are ultimately still inert objects or simply fiction. Dragons, however, actually impinge upon human consciousness even now, even beyond stories. They are not dead, stuffed exhibits, but chaos monsters that threaten the living through spiritual attack. Demons are part of our actual experience.

As I mentioned at the beginning of this book, dragons and other monsters appear in the Scriptures, and they do so partly because the humans who wrote the Scriptures experienced them. And because we believe that these humans wrote the Scriptures with the inspiration of the Holy Spirit, that means the Spirit led them to include these monsters in those texts. Even though we do not place stories and legends on the same level as the Scriptures—far from it—we can still see them as representing this same experience with the demonic, as well as attempts to deal with it. Inasmuch as these representations are consistent with the Scriptures (and not all are, or in every way), they also are the work of the Holy Spirit for us.

So why do these monsters exist, and why do they present themselves to us? Since they are demonic forces, it is essentially for the same reason that we saw in the previous chapter: God permits and even uses these beings to spur us to repentance. However, the suffering we experience under demonic attack doesn't only bring us to repentance; it doesn't only lead us to call upon God and increase our faithfulness to Him in our helplessness. Dragon stories, as Tolkien says, are not just about monsters; they are about the overthrowing of monsters. The victory of Christ and the saints over dragons can instill hope in us as we face these creatures ourselves. When we ponder the monsters of the Scriptures and of subsequent Christian tradition, this question and answer should always be in mind.

We've spent some time discussing the spiritual beings that inhabit our cosmos, so now let's explore the shape of the cosmos itself.

CHAPTER 4

Sacred Cosmology and Geography

And God said, "Let there be an expanse in the midst of the waters, and let it separate the waters from the waters." And God made the expanse and separated the waters that were under the expanse from the waters that were above the expanse. And it was so. And God called the expanse Heaven.

—Genesis 1:6–8a

It is right that any one beginning to narrate the formation of the world should begin with the good order which reigns in visible things. I am about to speak of the creation of heaven and earth, which was not spontaneous, as some have imagined, but drew its origin from God. What ear is worthy to hear such a tale?

—St. Basil the Great[1]

1 Saint Basil the Great, *Hexaemeron* I.1, trans. Blomfield Jackson, in *Nicene and Post-Nicene Fathers II*, eds. Philip Schaff and Henry Wace, vol. 8 (Peabody, MA: Hendrickson Publishers, 1999), 52.

THE EARLIEST KNOWN POETRY IN English is a hymn to the Creator, composed in Old English in the late seventh century. It came to the mind of an illiterate and rough shepherd who had been incapable of poetry or song and was ashamed of his incapacity. Yet in a vision, he heard the voice of God commanding him to sing of the creation. This is the hymn that came to him:

Now shall we hail heaven-kingdom's Guardian,
the might of the Measurer and His mind's counsel,
work of the Father glorious, as wonders for each He,
the Forever-Lord, founded their beginning.
He first made for men's sons
heaven for a roof, the holy Maker;
then middle-earth mankind's Guardian,
the Forever-Lord, fashioned after—
for men the Earth, Master almighty.[2]

The poet was St. Cædmon of Whitby, and St. Bede of Jarrow tells his story in his *Ecclesiastical History of the English People*. The poem, known as "Cædmon's Hymn," was one of the most popular poems in the Old English period, found in twenty-one manuscripts—more than any other poem of the time. In the poem, St. Cædmon describes heaven as a "roof" made by God, who is the guardian of the heavenly Kingdom. After making heaven, He makes *middangeard*, literally "middle-earth," and St. Cædmon in this context calls God "mankind's Guardian," the almighty Master, Measurer, and Forever-Lord who made the Earth for humanity.

This early medieval English Christian poem witnesses to how ancient people understood cosmology, which is the sense of how the cosmos is arranged. In the poem, we see two levels—the heavens and

2 This is my own translation from Old English.

the earth, a clear reference to Genesis 1:1. There is a third level, that the hymn does not mention, which ancient texts variously refer to as the deeps, the Abyss, or the underworld. Most ancient religious traditions and their texts, including the Scriptures, reference or assume this three-level cosmos.

In our time, the idea that heaven is above us and the underworld is below us can seem quaint, old-fashioned, even superstitious. We have been to outer space, and we have seen that there is no heaven up there beyond the atmosphere. We have dug very deep into the earth, and no one has found any evidence of an underworld. So how are we to understand what almost every culture everywhere believed until just a few centuries ago? Do we just reject it, along with all the narratives and texts that assume this cosmology? We will discuss how we receive this cosmology as modern people at the end of this chapter, but first, we should try to understand what exactly it means. If we are going to reject it, we should at least know what we are rejecting.

The Heavens

In many languages, the words for "sky" and "heaven" are the same word. In archaic English, *the heavens* has both these senses, and *heofon* in St. Cædmon's Old English meant both these things. In Greek, *ouranos* is both. In Latin, it is *caelum*. In biblical Hebrew, it is *shamayim*. In Arabic, it is *sama'*. In Lithuanian, it is *dangus*. In many other languages, if there are two words for these two concepts, they are related, such as the Russian *nebo* and *nebesa* or the Mandarin Chinese *tiānkōng* and *tiāntáng*.

The English word *sky* looks and sounds so different from *heaven* that it may not be clear why most languages have closely associated these two concepts. In modern English, *sky* is the visible blueness we see above us (thus, *sky blue*) and perhaps the space higher than we can reach (which is why we say that birds fly "in the sky" even though they are not in the blue part). *Sky* is a thirteenth-century borrowing from Old Norse, referring to the clouds or the region where the clouds are, which is why we use *sky* the way we do.

By contrast, modern English speakers envision *heaven* as a spiritual good place where some people go when they die, where God and the angels live. It is sometimes depicted as a silly place where people sit on clouds and play harps for eternity. Even though we don't tend to think of the sky and heaven as the same place, English speakers have a sense that heaven is "up there" somewhere, and the clouds in heavenly imagery support this sense, though they would not point to the sky itself as the location of heaven.

Yet we still tend to think this way when looking at ancient cosmology. In Genesis 11:4, for instance, when we consider that the builders of the Tower of Babel wanted its top to reach "the heavens," we may interpret this to mean that they thought God was "up there" somewhere, that they could reach Him if only they built their tower tall enough. But at what altitude is God exactly? Or at what level in the atmosphere does one pass from hovering above the earth to occupying the heavens? We have to conclude that ancient people were just ridiculous for making this connection.

To get a sense for how the concepts of the sky and heaven were actually joined in the minds of ancient people, let's look at how the Scriptures refer to heaven. Beginning with Genesis 1, God creates "the heavens and the earth" (1:1). He then creates an expanse (or "firmament") that He calls "heaven," which divides waters above and waters below (1:6–8). With this sense that heaven separates waters above and below, we already have a concept that is different from *sky* as we now use it.

Along with the making of light, which shines into the darkness and is separated out from it (Gen. 1:4), it is the creation of the heavens that begins the process of making structure for the cosmos, which up until then had been "without form and void" (Gen. 1:2)—unstructured and empty. With these basic structures put into place, a pattern emerges in which God first makes form and then fills it, thus overcoming the formlessness and emptiness. To fill this first structure, God goes on in Genesis 1:14–19 to create lights, which He sets in heaven—the sun and moon to rule the day and night, respectively, as well as the stars. We noted in chapter 2 that angels are closely associated with the heavenly lights, so when we read in Genesis about God filling the heavens with these lights that "rule" over the day and night, an array of constellations with the sun and moon in motion, we should think of that "ruling" happening in a very personal sense, instrumentally through the angelic powers.

This concept of heaven is now very different from our sky, which definitely does not include the sun, moon, and stars because we think of those as being above the sky, outside of the earth's atmosphere. Yet in verses 20–30, God creates birds and places them to fly in the heavens, which again suggests a concept like our modern "sky." From this general shape in Genesis 1, we get the sense that heaven is a kind of pressurized expanse that holds waters above and below. Birds can fly through it. It is not just air, however, because in its heights it includes the celestial lights, which are well beyond human reach. In essence, Genesis depicts heaven as a sort of dome over the earth, a "roof," as in St. Cædmon's poem.

The biblical image of heaven does not end with this material description, however. Later, Genesis refers to God as the "God of heaven" (Gen. 24:3, 7), a title that gets repeated throughout the Old Testament and then is used again in Revelation (Rev. 11:13, 16:11). Given that God is not actually visible in the sky, hovering somewhere above in His aerial realm (unlike the "sky god" of ancient pagan myth), now we are getting a different sense of heaven. It is not quite material. And as if to emphasize that God is not actually localized to heaven, it is said that "heaven and the highest heaven cannot contain [Him]" (1 Kin. 8:27).

In Genesis 28:10–17, the account of Jacob's dream in a place he would call *Bethel,* Jacob sees a stairway that reaches to heaven (28:12), and he identifies the place as the "house of God," the "gate of heaven" (28:17). No material reading of this experience would make sense. Jacob experiences access to God in some way, and his testimony is that the dwelling place of God is found through a gateway to heaven. He is not saying that God lives in the sky somewhere. Instead, he unites the imagery of the dome of the sky with the sense of the presence of God.

As St. John of Damascus tries to summarize what he sees in the Scriptures regarding heaven, as well as what the Church Fathers before him say, he gives several different models.[3] He begins by describing the material sense of heaven as a circular dome, but he also says that God is not bound by it:

> Heaven is that which contains visible and invisible created beings, for within it the intelligible [*noetic*] powers of the angels and all sensible things are enclosed and confined. Only the divine is uncircumscribed, filling all things and surrounding all things and confining all things, since it transcends all things and has created all things.

Clearly, the limited "sky god" of paganism is not God. Notice that St. John also says that heaven surrounds all created things, including the invisible creation such as the angels.

He goes on to say that the Scripture speaks of "heaven, 'the heaven of heavens,' and 'the heavens of heavens,'" and that St. Paul mentions being caught up to the "third heaven" (2 Cor. 12:2). From this, St.

---

3 *Exact Exposition,* bk. II, ch. 6.

John says that heaven can be identified as the "starless sphere" but also as the expanse or firmament that divides the waters. He notes that some say there are seven zones to heaven, some say that heaven is composed of material "delicate as smoke" or even water, and some say that heaven is a sphere that surrounds all the universe while others say it is a hemisphere (the dome image).

Saint John sees these various distinctions as all permissible within the language of the Old Testament Scriptures, and there is flexibility, too:

> And if you wish to take the seven zones [of the planetary spheres] as seven heavens, no harm is done to the word of truth. It is also customary in the Hebrew language to refer to heaven in the plural as "heavens." When Hebrew wished to say "heaven of heaven," it said "heavens of heavens," which indicates the heaven of heaven that is above the firmament and the waters that are above the vault of heaven, whether it is the air and the firmament, or the seven zones of the firmament, or the firmament itself that are spoken of in the plural in accordance with Hebrew usage.

Even though we can speak of heaven in these various ways and try to distinguish between the different usages, as you can see, he does not pick one material or even spiritual model for what heaven is, exactly. Indeed, after this complex discussion he concludes that "the heaven is greater than the earth, but we need not investigate the essence of the heaven, for it is quite beyond our knowledge." In the end, in understanding heaven, what really matters is what we experience, not devising taxonomic knowledge of the heavens. The roof of heaven is not simply an object made by God, but an object made by God *for humans.*

Saint John adds this word of caution to the end of his chapter on heaven:

> Nor should it be assumed that the heavens or the heavenly bodies are endowed with souls, for they are inanimate and insensate. Therefore, even if the divine Scripture says: "Let the heavens rejoice and the earth exult," it is inviting the angels in heaven and human beings on earth to rejoice. . . . By contemplating their beauty we glorify their maker as the supreme craftsman.

Why make this point? Saint John is warning us ultimately against idolatry, a warning the Scriptures delivered many times regarding the heavenly bodies, that we ought not to worship them (Deut. 4:19). But he is also showing us the purpose of our experience of the heavens, that by "contemplating their beauty we glorify their maker," which is exactly what we see in Cædmon's Hymn. The relationship of the heavens to humanity is ultimately to raise us up to God.

Middle-earth

From the title of this section, you can likely tell I am an unabashed J. R. R. Tolkien fan and occasional scholar. Tolkien did not invent the idea of "middle-earth," however. We saw that Cædmon's Hymn in the seventh century used the Old English *middangeard,* and the word also shows up in the late ninth- or early tenth-century poem "Christ," by Cynewulf, in the lines *Eala earendel, engla beorhtast / ofer middangeard monnum sended* ("Hail, daystar, brightest angel / over middle-earth to mankind sent"), which are the lines that inspired Tolkien to use the name for a continent on his fantasy world. Middle-earth is not a continent in pre-modern literature, however. It is simply the earth, and the name is found throughout Germanic literature in various forms: *Miðgarðr* ("Midgard") in Old Norse, *Middilgard* in Old Saxon, and *Midjungards* in Gothic.[4] The *-gard* ending is cognate with

4 Along with other Christian texts, the Old Saxon *Heliand* (a retelling of the

English *yard*, and it means "an enclosed space." Thus, these terms literally mean "an enclosed space in the middle."

What is the earth in the middle of? Ancient three-level cosmology conceives the earth as below the heavens but above the watery underworld. Thus, it is an enclosed space in the middle, bounded by the dome of the heavens. The creation of the earth itself is part of God's creation of structures for His cosmos. Thus, in Genesis 1:9–10, God separates the earth from the waters:

> And God said, "Let the waters under the heavens be gathered together into one place, and let the dry land appear." And it was so. God called the dry land Earth, and the waters that were gathered together he called Seas. And God saw that it was good.

It's not clear from these verses exactly what the relationship of the land to the water is. You get the sense that the waters are brought together, which then reveals dry land. If you look at a map with both land and sea on it, this is what appears—land in one place, water in another. Elsewhere in the Bible, though, the image gets more specific, with the land very clearly on top of the waters: "The earth is the LORD's and the fullness thereof, / the world and those who dwell therein, / for he has founded it upon the seas / and established it upon the rivers" (Ps. 24:1–2). Here we more clearly have the middle-earth image, with the heavens above and the waters below.

The earth does not merely float upon the waters but is supported by pillars that God set there (Ps. 75:3; 1 Sam. 2:8; Job 9:6), the "beams of his chambers on the waters" (Ps. 104:3), which reach down into the abysmal depths. What is beneath these pillars we are not told, but it is God Himself supporting them: "When the

Gospels in Germanic style) uses these forms, as does the Gothic Gospel of Luke, which translates the Greek *oikoumeni* as the "inhabited world."

earth totters, and all its inhabitants, / it is I who keep steady its pillars" (Ps. 75:3).

If that is how the earth relates to what is below, how does it relate to what is above? Saint John of Damascus speaks about this relationship of the heavenly bodies to the earth:

> On the fourth day God made the great luminary, which is the sun, to be the source and regulating principle of the day (for it is through the sun that the day is constituted, day being when the sun is over the earth, and the space of a day being the sun's course above the earth from east to west), and the lesser luminary, which is the moon, together with the stars, to be the source and regulating principle of the night and to illuminate it. It is night when the sun is below the earth, and the duration of a night is the sun's course below the earth from west to east.[5]

The model here is clearly of a flat earth around which the heavenly bodies move. The sun and other luminaries can be above or below the earth. This model is consistent with everything we've seen from the Scriptures.

Before we discuss the underworld, I can imagine that your incredulity might be growing here. Is it really true that pre-modern people believed in a flat earth, bounded with a dome, with the sun, moon, and stars circling above and below the earth? And if so, what about the modern scientific discoveries that the earth is roughly spherical? Haven't we seen it from outer space and even taken photographs of the earth, seen that it rotates on its axis, seen that it revolves around the sun? Does this mean that ancient cosmology is just superstitious garbage?

---

5 *Exact Exposition*, bk. II, ch. 7.

First, contrary to popular belief, the earth was not discovered only recently to be spherical. Greek philosophers posited it at least around the fifth century BC. Two hundred years later, astronomers proved it through calculation and even figured out its circumference. This should be no surprise, since if you look off in the direction of the horizon you can see an end to the land, yet if you walk in that direction, new objects begin to appear. The earth has to be curved for this effect to be possible. However, despite knowledge of the roundness of the earth, most people still spoke about it as though the three-level cosmology were true. Saint John of Damascus (an inheritor and student of Greek learning) lived in the eighth century, for instance, over a millennium after the discovery of the earth's roundness.

Were pre-modern people just stubborn, unwilling to accept new scientific knowledge? In some cases, that is no doubt true. In many cases, however, it is clear that people living in the same time and place believed in both cosmologies simultaneously—the flat-earth, three-level cosmology right alongside the beginnings of the round-earth cosmology with its complex relationship between earth and the luminaries.

We will discuss later how they could believe in both at the same time, but for now, let's ask this: Why did they keep speaking of the three-level cosmology even when they had evidence to the contrary? It is because they also had positive evidence that it was true. When you walk on the earth, it feels flat. You don't feel like you're walking on a ball. When you look up in the sky, you see the sun and moon, and from your point of view, they are rising and setting. We still speak this way, that the sun "rises" and "sets," even though the effect is created by the earth itself spinning.

This understanding of cosmology is phenomenological—it is what humans actually experience. Modern people might say that we are fooling ourselves with this cosmology, but that view requires imagining that something we do not experience is the truth while what we experience is not true. That mental imagination exercise is now very common, however, and we almost take it for granted. Yet when we do, we miss something important about what it means to be human, cutting off a direct apprehension of our real experiences. I am not lying to myself when I say that the sun rises.

There is also a theological basis for including experiential knowledge in our vision of the world—God made it for humans. The world is not an object for us to observe in a detached way but rather a series of relationships with humanity. The word *world* itself comes from roots meaning "man age," that is, the realm of humanity. God gave the world to Adam and Eve for them to fill and cultivate. He fashioned it for humankind, which means that He gave us our experiences of the world's structure. Our scientific exploration is also another form of knowledge, but it does not need to displace other ways of knowing.

Let's move on now to what is perhaps the most mysterious and difficult to understand level of ancient cosmology—the underworld.

The Underworld

When I think about how ancient cosmology is arranged, I sometimes remember how I once climbed the tallest mountain in the world. No, I don't mean Mount Everest, which is the *highest* mountain in the world—the one that reaches highest in the air, highest above sea level. I could never climb Everest. Rather, I mean I climbed the *tallest* mountain—Mount Lamlam. You might never have heard of Mount Lamlam, but that's because if you measure its height above sea level, which is 1,332 feet (406 meters), it's not much of a mountain. It's near the village of Agat on the Pacific Island of Guam, and it just barely qualifies as a mountain. Yet because the mountain is on Guam, it is geologically the top of a colossal drop in elevation, down more than 36,000 feet (11,000 meters) into the Mariana Trench, the deepest place in the world. (For comparison, Everest is 29,032 feet high.)

I lived in Santa Rita, the next village over, for five years, and climbed Lamlam once. Standing on top of Lamlam, even though it really is just a little mountain, we felt that we could touch the sky. Beneath our feet, however, were the roots of the deepest place on the whole planet. Because of the water pressure no human could ever swim that deep, even if they could hold their breath the whole way down. They would die long before they reached the bottom.

Ancient cosmology depicts what is under the earth as a vast watery abyss, which both surrounds the flat disc of the earth but also undergirds it. In this abyss, the pillars of the earth stand. The relationship of the abyss to humankind is mainly about death. This association with death makes immediate sense if you think about the experience of being drowned in the sea. Water in large amounts is profoundly dangerous to human beings. Even in our modern technological age, ships sink and are lost at sea. In the United States where I live, some four thousand people drown every year.

Consider also the sea itself—it is deep and powerful. Most people cannot even fathom its depths, and we can reach the deepest parts of the ocean only with highly specialized technology. Few have ever tried. In 1960, inside a powerfully armored submarine called the *Trieste*, Jacques Piccard and Don Walsh descended to the bottom of the Mariana Trench in a place called the Challenger Deep, spent twenty minutes there without taking any photographs because of the silt they stirred up, then ascended again. No one else has ever returned.

The association of the underworld with the watery depths is made most explicit in the story of Jonah, who is swallowed by the great sea monster and taken into the depths of the sea. There, Jonah calls out to God with this prayer:

> I called out to the Lord, out of my distress, / and he answered me; / out of the belly of Sheol I cried, / and you heard my voice. / For you cast me into the deep, / into the heart of the seas, / and the flood surrounded me; / all your waves and your billows / passed over me. (Jon. 2:2–3)

What is Sheol? In ancient Semitic religious texts, Sheol is the underworld of the dead. *Sheol* literally means "the grave." In this same prayer, Jonah also says, "Then I said, 'I am driven away / from your sight; / yet I shall again look / upon your holy temple'" (Jon. 2:4), which expresses the sense of separation from God as the experience of one who is in the underworld. He goes on:

> The waters closed in over me to take my life; / the deep surrounded me; / weeds were wrapped about my head / at the roots of the mountains. / I went down to the land / whose bars closed upon me forever; / yet you brought up my life from the pit, / O Lord my God. (Jon. 2:5–6)

Jonah again uses the imagery of being in the depths of the ocean, which here is located at "the roots of the mountains," reflecting the cosmology of the third level beneath the earth. He also describes his experience as being locked in a place where bars close permanently upon him. This place is also called "the pit," a bottomless hole from which one can never escape.

Jonah entered the underworld of death when a sea monster brought him there, but since it is under the ground, we have many possible entrances. Various religious traditions regarded other places, such as the Egyptian *Yam Suph*—the Sea of Reeds, through which Israel crossed in the Exodus—as entrances to the underworld. Watery places were not the only possible entrances, though—some traditions said that caves led to the underworld, such as the cave called the Devil's Throat, where Orpheus ventured to find his lost Eurydice. Burial places, where human bodies are placed underground or in caves, also participate in this imagery.

Humans experience the depths of the sea as not only deadly but also mysterious and off-limits. Most of humanity cannot reach it. This inscrutable inaccessibility is probably one of the reasons why the Bible refers so often to heaven and earth together—hundreds of times—but does not pair them with the underworld, even though that place of death was just as much a part of the biblical cosmology. Humanity experiences the heavens and the earth, but the underworld is a loathed place of foreboding.

The Scriptures also associate the heavens and earth with the realm of God, who is not only present in the heavens and earth but is also their Lord (e.g., Gen. 14:19, 22, 24:3, etc.). And while God cannot be said to be wholly absent from anywhere, being present in some sense even in the underworld (Ps. 139:7–8), as we saw with Jonah, the underworld also carries a sense of separation from God. Even more, however, the underworld is not depicted as the realm of God, even though He is the ruler over all. He is not the God of the dead (Matt. 22:32; Mark 12:27).

Is there a god of the dead? In the Scriptures, the one who has the power of death is the devil (Heb. 2:14). God gave this power to the devil when He stripped all other powers from him in Genesis 3:14, where He condemns the serpent (the fallen seraph that is the devil) to eat dust. What does dust have to do with death? Adam is himself formed from dust (Gen. 2:7), and being made of dust from the ground, when he begins to die, he is condemned to return to dust (Gen. 3:19). The serpent eating dust is thus an image of swallowing up the dead. It is for this reason that Christian iconography features an image called the "Hellmouth," which is a gigantic serpentine figure swallowing the bodies of humanity. In many places, the Scriptures say that the hungry Sheol (Is. 5:14) "swallows" the dead, the ground opening up to receive them (e.g., Num. 16:30–33; Prov. 1:12).

This image of the voracious Sheol is not merely a poetic personification. Sheol is not only the place of the dead but also possibly the god of the dead in Semitic religion, including Semitic paganism. *Sheol* may possibly be derived from the Akkadian name *Shuwala,* a death goddess in the Hurrian tradition. Whether the linguistic derivation is true or not, it is clear that many ancient religious traditions use a name for their primary death god that is the same as the name of the underworld where the deity rules. The insatiable Sheol is also associated with the demon Abbadon (Job 26:6; Prov. 15:11, 27:20), a demon of destruction and also the name of the place of destruction. In Greek paganism, the god Hades rules Hades. The Norse goddess Hel (or Hela) rules Hell. The Finnish god Tuoni rules Tuonela.

Others associate the death god with the souls of the dead, such as the Baltic god Velnias (or Veles), who rules over *vėlės* (souls). Chinese divine judges called Yánwáng rule over Dìyù, the underworld of the dead, judging the souls that enter. To be dead is to be in the power of the god of death. Numerous pagan death-deities' names are simply also the language's word for "death," such as the Canaanite Mot, the Roman Mors, or the Greek Thanatos (or Thanos). Revelation 9:11 makes explicit the rule of a demonic death god over the pit of death: "They have as king over them the angel of the bottomless pit. His name in Hebrew is Abaddon, and in Greek he is called Apollyon."

In the deepest part of the underworld is a place called by the Greek name *Tartarus,* where the most wicked demons are imprisoned. Saint Peter mentions angels who sinned before the Flood of Noah and were cast into Tartarus (2 Pet. 2:4–5), a story which somewhat parallels the Greek pagan tale of the Titans, who were similarly imprisoned in the lowest depths of Hades.

The underworld can be a frightening thing to ponder, not only because it is often depicted as torturous but primarily because it is understood as oblivion. For many ancient religions, souls who go there gradually fade into nothingness until the living forget them, giving rise to the pagan practice of "feeding" the graves of heroes with sacrificed blood to help them continue to live and perhaps communicate with the living (a practice that appears in Homer's *The Odyssey*).

This sense of death as being forgotten also gave rise to the Christian practice of praying "memory eternal" for our Christian dead. The "memory" we pray about is not the memory of living Christians; we are not asking God to make sure people on earth never forget about the person. After all, the living eventually forget most humans who have ever lived. Rather, only God has an eternal memory, and we ask Him to remember us and our departed. His memory of us is therefore seen, in a sense, as sustaining us so that we will never be subject to oblivion in the dark underworld.

The Modern Mind and the Mountain of God

I once read somewhere that Christianity needs to update its cosmology, that modern Christians cannot believe in a three-level model of the created world, given what we now know about the earth, the solar system, the galaxy, and so on. I cannot imagine what it would actually look like for modern Christians to do this, however, given how much of the Christian story is based on this imagery. To imagine one major example, consider the descent of Christ into Hades, which the Orthodox Church and other Christian traditions celebrate on Holy Saturday. By dying, Christ enters the underworld. He stands at the barred gates of Hades and demands the devil—the death god—to come out. He smashes the doors inward, defeats the devil, then enters into Hades and draws out the souls of the righteous who had been imprisoned there.

I have an icon of this very scene, modeled on icons found in medieval English illuminated manuscripts. The icon shows Christ standing at the Hellmouth, a great, green serpentine head that yawns open, where numerous souls are standing, Adam first among them. His right hand has hold of Adam by the wrist, while beneath His feet are the broken doors of the underworld. Beneath those doors is the dark, demonic figure of the devil, bound in chains, whose mouth is being poked by the bannered Cross that Christ holds in His left hand. Meanwhile, an angel stands beside Christ and pokes the devil in the chest with a long lance. The sun and the moon, both with faces indicating the angels who steward them, look on in amazement.

We can think of other examples of Christian imagery that depend on ancient cosmology. Consider when Christ ascends into heaven and is enthroned at the right hand of God (Mark 16:19). If God's throne and dwelling place is not in some sense up in heaven, then where did Christ go, exactly? Or consider when Ezekiel 28:13–16 depicts the devil as a guardian cherub who is cast down from Eden, the holy Mountain of God. Without that sense of the divine being "up" and the demonic being "down," how does this story make sense?

It is clear that the whole story of Christianity simply does not work without the ancient cosmological model. We cannot revise our cosmology without turning Christianity into something completely new. So does that mean that modern materialist atheism has defeated Christianity because of its erroneous cosmology? No.

To understand why I say no to this question, let's use the example of the Mountain of God. I mentioned earlier that Ezekiel 28 depicts Eden, the Garden of God, as being on a mountain. This identification of Eden as being in a high place is perhaps not obvious from the Genesis description we're probably more familiar with, but if you look at Genesis 2:10–14, you will see it says that four rivers flow out of Eden, watering the garden. This imagery for Paradise not only indicates its abundant fertility but also provides a clue that it is a high place, which is necessary for rivers to flow downward. Ezekiel 28:14 calls this the "holy mountain of God," while verse 16 calls it the "mountain of God" from which the devil is cast out "as a profane thing." So from the Scriptural evidence, the Paradise of Eden is a garden on a mountain.

This association of a mountain with the divine is found throughout ancient religious sources, and it is why so many temples and shrines are on mountains and why people sometimes create artificial sacred mountains, namely ziggurats. If you want to have an encounter with your god, you ascend a mountain, often a particular mountain where the god is said to live. Furthermore, especially in the ancient Near East where so much of the land is desert, gardens are also associated with the divine, since they are places of abundant life and fertility. The biblical Eden fits into this pattern, but so do pagan places like the Hanging Gardens of Babylon, which are a man-made garden-ziggurat.

Identifying Eden as the Mountain of God is not the end of this story, however. If we continue to track the Mountain of God in the Bible, we will discover the key to why ancient, three-level cosmology is neither something that Christianity needs to discard (thereby changing Christianity fundamentally) nor is it the checkmate that ends the game for us.

Exodus 3 uses the phrase *mountain of God* for Mount Horeb, near where Moses was sojourning in Midian. Here Moses sees God and speaks with Him at the Burning Bush. God tells him that Moses would serve Him "on this mountain" (Ex. 3:12). Exodus 4:27 and 18:5 again call Horeb "the mountain of God." So is Horeb the Mountain of God? Is Horeb actually Eden? By the time we get to Exodus 24, Moses is approaching God on the mountain, where His glory dwells (Ex. 24:16). Again, we see the phrase *the mountain of God* (24:13), but this mountain is not Horeb. Now, Moses is on Mount Sinai (24:16)! On Sinai, Moses offers up sacrifices to God, serving Him (24:5–8).

But didn't God say that Moses was supposed to serve Him at "this mountain," meaning Horeb?

The Scriptures also call Zion "the holy mountain" or "the mountain of the Lord" (Ps. 48:1, Ps. 99; Is. 66:20; Mic. 4:2; Joel 3:17, etc.). Psalm 68:15 calls a mountain in Bashan, north of Israel, "the mountain of God" (possibly Tabor or Hermon). Saint Peter refers to Tabor, where the Transfiguration of Christ took place, as "the holy mountain" (2 Pet. 1:18).

What are we to make of this? Are the biblical writers confused on the location of the holy Mountain of God? Do they think all these places are possible locations of Eden? Did Moses make a mistake by serving God at Sinai rather than Horeb? To answer these questions, let's consider what all these mountains have in common: they are all places where God's people go to meet Him, to serve Him, to worship Him, to encounter Him, and to hear from Him. The Mountain of God is a kind of spiritual geography that overlays material geography. Thus, there is but one Mountain of God, but it can be ascended in many places. That is why God could tell Moses to serve Him on "this mountain," and "this mountain" becomes Sinai even though it was Horeb when God gave the command.

Thus, sacred geography and cosmology do not fundamentally contradict the material cosmology of the modern age. Remember that ancient Greeks already believed in a round world, and even with this knowledge, Christians continued to describe their story in terms of three-level cosmology. While some writers clearly envisioned the world *only* with three-level cosmology, it is possible to believe in both cosmologies at the same time. Each cosmology simply describes a different experience of the world. They do not need to be compatible with each other because they are not fundamentally trying to describe the same thing.

Both are about experiences including the material world, however. It is not that the round-world cosmology is about materiality and three-level cosmology is about a "spiritual" (read: imaginary) existence. Rather, Orthodox Christianity holds both material and spiritual experience together in association, as in this hymn from the *Octoechos*: "The Cross was fixed upon the earth, and touched the Heavens, not because the wood reached unto the height, but because Thou, Who fillest all things, wast upon it. Lord, glory be to Thee."[6]

This hymn references and associates both the "height" and the "Heavens." Nonetheless, the Cross reaches the Heavens only because Christ, the one who is both God and man, uncreated and created, material and immaterial at the same time, is upon it. The hymn is not saying that the Cross is very tall because Christ is on it. Rather, through Christ's presence the Cross participates in the Heavens, because Heaven is the experience of being with God. At the same time, Christ fills all things, which is a cosmological possibility we cannot really even comprehend. Nonetheless, we continue to reach up to the heights of the Heavens through our ritual participation in Him.

Thus, Christians often have built their churches on high places, and even those built in low places or plains traditionally include elevation within them, even if it is only one step up from the nave (the central worship space in a church) to the altar. Why do they do that? Because when the priest ascends toward the altar, there he continues with all the people to fulfill the command of God to worship Him on "this mountain," the Mountain of God that becomes present at that moment, overlaying the material geography with a spiritual geography.

6 *Octoechos* (Brookline, MA: Holy Transfiguration Monastery, 2019), 149.

CHAPTER 5

The City of Man and the City of God

As we have heard, so have we seen / in the city of the Lord *of hosts, / in the city of our God, / which God will establish forever.*

—Psalm 48:8

The Church is not of this world, as her Lord, Christ, was also not of the world. But He was in this world, having "humbled" Himself to the condition of that world which He came to save and to redeem. The Church also had to pass through a process of the historical kenosis, in the exercise of her redemptive mission in the world. Her purpose was not only to redeem men out of this world, but also to redeem the world itself.

—Fr. Georges Florovsky[1]

1 Georges Florovsky, "Antinomies of Christian History: Empire and Desert," in *The Collected Works of Georges Florovsky*, vol. II, *Christianity and Culture* (Belmont, MA: Nordland Publishing Company, 1974), 96.

In the previous chapter we spoke about the spiritual geography that overlays material geography. In this chapter we will discuss the effects of spiritual reality on humankind's life in this world. What does the world look like when this unseen reality interacts with it? What does this mean for civilization? We will therefore begin with Paradise.

Eden

The second chapter of Genesis tells how God made Adam and placed him in Eden:

> When no bush of the field was yet in the land and no small plant of the field had yet sprung up—for the LORD God had not caused it to rain on the land, and there was no man to work the ground, and a mist was going up from the land and was watering the whole face of the ground—then the LORD God formed the man of dust from the ground and breathed into his nostrils the breath of life, and the man became a living creature. (Gen. 2:5–7)

We recall from the previous chapter how the world was barren and chaotic until God gave it shape and filled it with life. Here we see this barrenness expressed as a dry land without even plant life. A mist goes up, and in the midst of this, God forms man from the dust of the ground, breathing life into his nostrils. He then makes the place appointed for Adam:

> And the LORD God planted a garden in Eden, in the east, and there he put the man whom he had formed. And out of the ground the LORD God made to spring up every tree that is pleasant to the sight and good for food. The tree of life was in the midst of the garden, and the tree of the knowledge of good and evil. (Gen. 2:8–9)

God plants Eden "in the east," which is not a location so much as an invocation of spiritual geography—the Scriptures say God comes "from the east" and lives "in the east" (e.g., Is. 24:15; Ez. 11:23, 43:2–4; Hos. 13:15). This spiritual location for Eden means that God is planting this garden where He Himself dwells. It is His presence that makes this place what it is. Note also that God "put the man whom he had formed" into Eden. Adam is not made from Eden but from the barrenness outside it; then God places him into the fertile garden.

In the previous chapter, I discussed how ancient peoples approached their gods on mountains and in gardens, and we saw how Eden is both. It fits into the general pattern of ancient Near Eastern narrative for encountering the divine. That does not mean that when Moses was writing Genesis he simply derived his narrative from pagan sources. For one thing, as Christians, we believe that God revealed what is in Genesis to Moses on Sinai. Perhaps more importantly, Genesis actually subverts the pagan narratives in a number of key ways.

A temple is the place where ancient people met their gods, and therefore pagan creation narratives are essentially the stories of the building of a temple. How did that narrative work? In most of these stories, the god forms a garden or mountain and humans build a temple in it, a place for their god to dwell. They then place an idol of the god—usually a statue image—into the temple. They performed a ceremony called the "opening of the nostrils" or sometimes "the opening of the eyes," and through this ritual the god's spirit was understood to be breathed into the idol, making the idol a body for the god, essentially trapping him inside. The human worshipers would then wash, clothe, and feed the idol, hoping to get from the god what they desired in exchange for this service of hospitality.

In Genesis 2, we see something quite similar, except God Himself builds the sacred space, and He places an image in the midst of that sacred space, an image of Himself (Gen. 1:27). It is not a lifeless idol, however, but a living man, into whom has been breathed not a god who is trapped there and available for control, but rather the "breath of life," God's Spirit freely inhabiting man and enlivening him for communion. God then takes care of this image of His, providing everything to him freely. If idolatry is about satisfying human desires by making deals with a god, then God's design is about His freely given providence for humans through communion.

Thus, we already see a significant contrast between the pagan stories that ancient people would have known and what they heard in the revelation when God spoke to Moses on Sinai. God is using the imagery of ancient religions to express His revelation to Moses, but He is also subverting it. The similarities are important, but so are the dissimilarities. In this storytelling, we thus see a pattern played out that we find throughout the Scriptures and subsequent Christian tradition—God's redemption of the world as it is. The people of Israel and pagans don't live in two different worlds. Rather, God's redemptive work renews the one world that actually exists and reveals it as belonging truly to Him.

Eden also is called *Paradise*, a word that we often think of as a synonym for *heaven*, which we might envision as the place where God is. (As we saw in the previous chapter, that is not really wrong, though it is incomplete.) We get this sense of Paradise from verses such as Luke 23:43, where Christ tells the thief on the cross that he would be with Him "in Paradise," or in 2 Corinthians 12:3, where St. Paul describes his mystical vision as being "caught up into Paradise." Yet we also see *Paradise* used in Revelation 2:7b: "To the one who conquers I will grant to eat of the tree of life, which is in the Paradise of God." Eating of the tree of life is a reference to Eden, and so we can see that Eden, the Mountain of God, heaven, and Paradise are really all the same place.

Yet the word *Paradise* is itself a kind of redemption because it does not have a biblical origin but rather comes out of Persian paganism.

It is from the Proto-Iranian (the earliest form of Persian) word *parā-daiĵah,* which came via Persian into Greek as *paradeisos* and thence into Latin and French, then into English as *paradise.* It originally meant "a walled enclosure," and its earliest uses certainly were within pagan contexts. When Greek borrowed it from Persian, it referred to the massive, sacred walled gardens of the Achaemenid Persian Empire, which featured four waterways coming to a point at the center. When the Old Testament was translated into Greek, *paradeisos* referred to Eden. The New Testament uses that same word and also applies it to the heavenly experience with God in Eden, itself a garden with four rivers flowing outward. Thus, by the use of *Paradise,* the Scriptures are not simply importing a pagan concept but using a known image to describe the setting for humankind's experience of God on earth.

Humanity's placement in Eden was not merely to give them a kind of permanent vacation in a lush environment, which is what we might imagine when we use *paradise* to describe, for instance, tropical islands for a warm getaway in the winter. Rather, God gave Adam and Eve work to do when He placed them in Paradise:

> So God created man in his own image, / in the image of God he created him; / male and female he created them.
>
> And God blessed them. And God said to them, "Be fruitful and multiply and fill the earth and subdue it, and have dominion over the fish of the sea and over the birds of the heavens and over every living thing that moves on the earth." (Gen. 1:27–28)

This two-part command of fertility ("be fruitful and multiply and fill the earth") and cultivation ("subdue [the earth]") directly parallels God's own actions in the creation. We saw how God first gave the earth structure, taming the chaos, then how He filled that structure with life, creating plants and animals, and finally humans. Humankind therefore is to do the same structuring, cultivating the earth not only in the sense of agriculture but more broadly in terms of the structuring that is beautification and civilization. And they are also to fill the earth with life, not only through human fertility in having children but with all kinds of life, both literally and figuratively.

Generally speaking, Adam's emphasis was on cultivation or structuring, which is why his first act along these lines was to name the animals (Gen. 2:19–20). Eve's emphasis was on fertility, which is why God created her when He found that no animal would "fit" (i.e., for reproduction) with Adam (Gen. 2:20–24). These are not really separate tasks, however. Adam and Eve needed each other for their primary tasks, and God called both to participate in both tasks. Also, He gave the commands "to *them*," not to each or to one alone. We also should not reduce their tasks to "building" and "childbirth." Cultivation has an almost infinite sense of application, for everything from architecture and engineering to agriculture, from philosophy and theology to storytelling. Likewise, fertility is not only about giving birth to children and raising them, but about filling all things with life and beauty.

Again, though, God gave these two commands to all of humanity, and the Scriptures repeat them several times. We should not take these emphases as simply playing to gender stereotypes, because Scripture does not sharply distinguish them. Furthermore, these tasks enable humans to participate in the creative, life-giving work of God Himself. Not only did God design this for Eden, He commissioned humans to expand Eden outward, to make the whole cosmos into Paradise. Eden and its expansion were God's models for human civilization.

All is lost, however, when Adam and Eve eat of the Tree of the Knowledge of Good and Evil, fruit they were not yet ready for. They disobeyed the commandment God had given them, trying to take what the Church Fathers say God ultimately would have given them, but they were yet too immature for it.

The Rise of Civilization

When Adam and Eve fall, having transgressed God's commandment, they receive the consequence of death, which is a mercy from God that enables their repentance,[2] and God drives them out of Eden and cuts them off from the Tree of Life (Gen. 3:19, 22–24). Adam and Eve lost God's design for humankind, which was to experience His presence and live with Him in communion in everlasting life. Furthermore, God did not withdraw their two tasks of fertility and cultivation as commands, but what has happened has made them more difficult, with Eve experiencing pain in childbirth and Adam's agricultural work becoming painful and onerous. Genesis 3:16–19 refers to these consequences of sin as a "curse."

As the curse sets into the world, human civilization takes a turn for the worse. The Bible's story of human civilization does not continue with Adam and Eve, however, nor with their son Seth (from whom Noah eventually will descend), but rather with Cain, who killed his brother Abel. In other words, humankind's model of civilization begins with a murderer.

Genesis 4 details the beginnings of what humanity would recognize as civilization—the founding of a city and the development of technology and culture:

> Cain knew his wife, and she conceived and bore Enoch. When [Enoch] built a city, he called the name of the city according to the

2 See the discussion around St. John of Damascus's comments in ch. 2 about why humankind's mortal corporeality is necessary for repentance.

> name of his son.[3] To Enoch was born Irad, and Irad fathered Mehujael, and Mehujael fathered Methushael, and Methushael fathered Lamech. (Gen. 4:17–18)[4]

At the beginning of this passage, the first city is built. In most translations, one gets the impression that Cain builds the first city and names it after his son Enoch. But the Hebrew is actually ambiguous here, with only the pronoun "he" designated as the one who built the city and called it after the name of his son.

In historical context, however, it makes more sense to read this as Enoch building the first city and then naming it for his son, whom the following verse identifies as Irad. What is that context, and why does this matter? In Mesopotamian tradition, the first city in the world is named *Eridu*. The name *Irad* itself means "city of dominion," and it is etymologically cognate with *Eridu*. This matters because, if we read it this way, Genesis embeds the Cain civilization narrative into ancient pagan traditions, a pattern we have already seen several times.

Local Sumerian pagan mythology said that the water god Enki founded Eridu, and he lived there within Abzu, a spring from which water flowed that brought life to the whole earth. You can see the obvious similarity here to Eden, the source of the four rivers that water all life on earth. By using this Eridu reference, therefore, the

---

3 In the ESV (from which I otherwise took this translation), the reading of verse 17 is "Cain knew his wife, and she conceived and bore Enoch. When he built a city, he called the name of the city after the name of his son, Enoch." Most English translations read this way. I am not a Hebrew scholar, but upon consultation with Fr. Stephen De Young, I have adjusted the translation to what you see here. Why will become apparent further on, but I acknowledge that this is nonstandard.

4 The names *Enoch* and *Lamech* also appear in the genealogy of Seth leading up to Noah (Gen. 5), but they are not the same men.

Bible is depicting the first city built by humanity as a kind of false Eden, a mockery of what God had made.

A false Eden represents a significant theme in the Scriptures—the attempt by human beings to make for themselves that which God had already given them or was going to give them. This theme is not about humans growing up and striking out on their own, but it is rather about breaking away from communion with God to try to take something on independently, which we saw with the taking of the fruit of the Tree of the Knowledge of Good and Evil.

The tale of the beginnings of human civilization continues:

> And Lamech took two wives. The name of the one was Adah, and the name of the other Zillah. Adah bore Jabal; he was the father of those who dwell in tents and have livestock. His brother's name was Jubal; he was the father of all those who play the lyre and pipe. Zillah also bore Tubal-cain; he was the forger of all instruments of bronze and iron. The sister of Tubal-cain was Naamah. (Gen. 4:19–22)

Here we see the rise of nomadic animal husbandry, music, and metallurgy, the first human technologies. How can these be evil? Why associate them with Cain? Probably the most obviously problematic technology here is metallurgy, the making of "instruments of bronze and iron." What kinds of instruments? This of course is a reference to weapons. As with many kinds of technology, the first thing that humanity developed with metallurgy was ways to kill each other.

It is perhaps harder to see what the problem with animal husbandry might be. This shift from hunting wild game to keeping livestock is one of the developments that enabled the amassing of wealth. When animals are controlled rather than tracked down, the possibility opens up of some people having more than others.

But what could possibly be wrong with music? We find a clue in the word *music* itself, which ultimately derives from the Greek phrase *Mousiki techni*, "art of the Muses." The ancient world believed that this art was given by divine beings—in the pagan Greek case, the Muses, who were the source of all knowledge regarding literature, science, and the arts. The word *muse* in English has come to be so common now to refer merely to inspiration that we may not realize it was a reference to goddesses. We might get some sense of how this would have sounded to ancient peoples, though, if we refer to electrical engineering, for instance, as the "art of Zeus," from the Greek god associated with thunder and lightning.

Saint Irenaeus of Lyons makes reference to fallen angels giving knowledge of such things, which were

> teachings of wickedness, in that they brought them the virtues of roots and herbs, dyeing in colours and cosmetics, the discovery of rare substances, love-potions, aversions, amours, concupiscence, constraints of love, spells of bewitchment, and all sorcery and idolatry hateful to God; by the entry of which things into the world evil extended and spread, while righteousness was diminished and enfeebled.[5]

This reflects a belief in the ancient world that the knowledge of *techni* came from spirits. *Techni* means the arts, broadly defined, which included not only what the modern world calls "art" but also what we would call medicine, engineering, and so on—things that humans make. (*Techni* is the origin of our word *technology*.) Music therefore is a *techni* given originally by demons, and its most ancient associations are especially with seduction and sorcery. As with the

---

5 Saint Irenaeus of Lyons, *The Proof of the Apostolic Preaching*, trans. J. Armitage Robinson (London: Macmillan, 1920), sec.18, https://www.tertullian.org/fathers/irenaeus_02_proof.htm.

rise of animal husbandry and metallurgy, it is about control over other humans.

This same theme of the demonic origin of technology is represented in the Jewish text 1 Enoch, which gives the names of various demons who grant different kinds of knowledge:

> And Azaz'el taught the people (the art of) making swords and knives, and shields, and breastplates; and he showed to their chosen ones bracelets, decorations, (shadowing of the eye) with antimony, ornamentation, the beautifying of the eyelids, all kinds of precious stones and all coloring tinctures and alchemy. And there were many wicked ones and they committed adultery and erred, and all their conduct became corrupt. Amasras taught incantation and the cutting of roots; and Armaros the resolving of incantations; and Baraqiyal astrology and Kokarer'el (the knowledge of) the signs and Tam'elk taught the seeing of the stars, and Asder'el taught the course of the moon as well as the deception of man. And (the people) cried and their voice reached unto heaven. (1 Enoch 8)[6]

As you can see, this divine source of technological knowledge does not only apply to music but to all these advancements. Perhaps the most famous example in the English-speaking world is the gift of fire to humanity from the Titan Prometheus.

Thus, we see that the rise of technology in Cain's line that Genesis 4 describes is not meant as a technological history, i.e., a list of inventors. Rather, Genesis is making use of this ancient association of the rise of technology with fallen divine beings to make a point about the nature of the wickedness of Cain and his offspring—it comes from cooperation with demons. That is why St. Irenaeus says that with the

---

6 1 Enoch, in *The Old Testament Pseudepigrapha*, ed. James H. Charlesworth, vol. 1 (Peabody, MA: Hendrickson Publishers, 1983), 16.

proliferation of technology "the affairs of wickedness were propagated to overflowing."

Babel

In the Scriptures, the city of Babylon, historically the capital of the Neo-Babylonian Empire (626–539 BC), is an image of the fallenness of human civilization. Before we get to this city, however, we get the story of a civilization called *Babel.* Babel is first referenced in Genesis 10:8–10, which notes it as the kingdom of a giant hunter called Nimrod, and its story unfolds in the following chapter:

> Now the whole earth had one language and the same words. And as people migrated from the east, they found a plain in the land of Shinar and settled there. And they said to one another, "Come, let us make bricks, and burn them thoroughly." And they had brick for stone, and bitumen for mortar. Then they said, "Come, let us build ourselves a city and a tower with its top in the heavens, and let us make a name for ourselves, lest we be dispersed over the face of the whole earth." And the LORD came down to see the city and the tower, which the children of man had built. And the LORD said, "Behold, they are one people, and they have all one language, and this is only the beginning of what they will do. And nothing that they propose to do will now be impossible for them. Come, let us go down and there confuse their language, so that they may not understand one another's speech." So the LORD dispersed them from there over the face of all the earth, and they left off building the city. Therefore its name was called Babel, because there the LORD confused the language of all the earth. And from there the LORD dispersed them over the face of all the earth. (Gen. 11:1–9)

Babel is connected here (via pun) with *balal,* a Hebrew word meaning "confusion," but its origin is the Assyrian *Bab-ilu,* "gate of a god."

Why would it be called that? We have good reason to believe that the tower being built in the center of Babel was a ziggurat, a step-pyramid structure designed to be an artificial mountain on which people may meet and worship gods. (See the previous chapter for more on the relationship between mountains and worship.)

Thus, the tower "with its top in the heavens" was not so tall that it literally reached the sky, which is where God is. Sometimes, one hears the story interpreted this way, that the tower builders thought they could reach God just by building a very tall tower, as though God is at some particular altitude. Keeping ancient cosmology in mind, however, we know that a tower whose top is in the heavens is designed rather to be a place where you could reach your god through ritual means. That is why this city has a name that means "gate of a god," because the ziggurat served as that gate.

We will talk more about how worship works in the next chapter, but for our purposes here, we will note that ancient people used ziggurats for idolatry. We mentioned earlier how people used idols to draw gods into them so that the gods might be trapped and controlled. Thus, the tower in Babel was built to draw God Himself (or perhaps a lesser god) down so that the people might use the religious technology of idolatry. Through this, they would "make a name for [themselves]," not only preventing their dispersion but rising up in greatness. It was a scheme to become the literal and figurative height of human civilization, in which "nothing that they propose to do will now be impossible for them."

As Genesis 11 relates, God does of course descend to the tower, but instead of submitting to enter into the idol in the ziggurat and participate in their blasphemous scheme, he scatters the Babel civilization through confusing their languages. In Orthodox Tradition, Pentecost in the Book of Acts reverses this scattering, where the apostles gain the ability to be heard in any language and all humankind is invited to reunite by entering the Church.

So what is Babel? It is the continuation of the story of the civilization of Cain, which becomes more wicked as time goes by, acquiring demonic knowledge and then finally attempting to control God Himself. This ultimate blasphemy is what destroys the city.

The Babel story follows Genesis 10, which is the genealogical story of the seventy nations that descend from Noah and his sons and fill the earth. Genesis 11 is not simply what happens next, however, but instead it tells the story of the growth and spread of human civilization from another angle. So the stories really are about the same thing—the scattering of the nations and their descent into greatest wickedness. That this is so becomes apparent from clues found elsewhere in the Bible. Deuteronomy 32:8, for example, refers to the Genesis 11 story: "When the Most High gave to the nations their inheritance, / when he divided mankind, / he fixed the borders of the peoples / according to the number of the sons of God."

There is an important note on translation here: *sons of God* is the reading from the Hebrew of the Dead Sea Scrolls. The Masoretic Text that many Protestant Bibles use instead reads "sons of Israel," which is an anachronism that makes no sense because Israel did not exist at this point in the narrative. The Greek Old Testament texts render this *angelon theou*, "angels of God." In other words, when God divided up the nations at the Babel event, He assigned them angelic beings called "sons of God" to govern them.[7] Why would He do that? Because after the Flood, He promised He would never destroy the earth this way again (Gen. 9:8–17). (The Flood was an effect of being in God's presence while greatly wicked, "death by holiness.") Because wickedness was again multiplying, God withdrew His direct presence to spare humankind, but He assigned them angels to serve as their patrons and protectors, one for each of the nations.

---

7 You can find this interpretation, among other places, in St. Irenaeus of Lyons, *Against Heresies* III.12.9; St. Justin Martyr, *Dialogue with Trypho* 131; and St. Victorinus, *Commentary on the Apocalypse* 9.13–14.

Traditional Orthodox icons of the Tower of Babel depict this assignment. In the center you see the tower, reaching up to the heavens. In front of the tower are three angels representing the authority of God, sending the nations away in every direction, giving to each one a scroll from a basket in front of them. The scrolls represent the languages of the nations. On the left and right you see men walking away from the tower, each dressed in the national garb of one nation or another, carrying their scrolls. Each man has an angel directly above and behind him, accompanying him on his way.[8]

The story does not end there, as Deuteronomy 32:16–17 relates:

> They stirred him to jealousy with strange gods; / with abominations they provoked him to anger. / They sacrificed to demons that were no gods, / to gods they had never known, / to new gods that had come recently, / whom your fathers had never dreaded.

These "new gods," the demons the people worshiped, were in fact the angelic patrons that God had assigned to the nations. They became fallen angels, and they cemented their relationship with their nations through the practice of idolatry. The descent of human civilization into wickedness was now total, with the people worshiping spirits other than the Most High God. This story is the biblical account of the rise of paganism, with which human civilization is completely bound up.

Babylon

How does Babel relate to Babylon? Most English Bibles don't make apparent that the Hebrew transliterated in Genesis 10–11 as *Babel* is

---

8 Given what I wrote above, it should be no surprise that churches that include this icon often juxtapose the icon of Pentecost in the corresponding symmetrical position in the church.

also rendered *Babylon* in other places. So the Scriptures use the same name for both the city with the tower in the center and also the city we will see again later where people like the prophet Daniel lived.

Babylon is of course a literal civilization that, among other things, deports the people of Israel from their land and where a number of the prophetic narratives of the Old Testament occur. It is also, however, a biblical symbol, bound up with idolatry and wickedness. God will therefore destroy this Babylon. We see this in the Revelation to St. John, where an angel says in the vision: "Fallen, fallen is Babylon the great, she who made all nations drink the wine of the passion of her sexual immorality" (Rev. 14:8). We also read: "The great city was split into three parts, and the cities of the nations fell, and God remembered Babylon the great, to make her drain the cup of the wine of the fury of his wrath" (Rev. 16:19). The city is "Babylon the great, mother of prostitutes and of earth's abominations" (Rev. 17:5).

The Babylon imagery of Revelation is aimed toward its destruction, yet notice that Babylon is not merely one city or even one empire, but rather that which intoxicates the nations with sexual immorality, which throughout the Scriptures is often associated with idolatry. Babylon is the ultimate symbol of human civilization, suffused with idolatry, self-serving people, and all kinds of wickedness. If sin were embodied as a city, that city is Babylon. Yet while Babylon made the world drink its cup of immorality, the cup of wrath that God gave Babylon to drink was His justice, which he brought against the city in order to end its evil.

God's destruction of Babylon comes to its fullness in Revelation 18, where an angel again cries out:

> "Fallen, fallen is Babylon the great! / She has become a dwelling place for demons, / a haunt for every unclean spirit, / a haunt for every unclean bird, / a haunt for every unclean and detestable beast. / For all nations have drunk / the wine of the passion of her sexual

> immorality, / and the kings of the earth have committed immorality with her, / and the merchants of the earth have grown rich from the power of her luxurious living." (Rev. 18:2–3)

The kings of the earth cry out, "Alas! Alas! You great city, / you mighty city, Babylon! / For in a single hour your judgment has come" (18:10), while merchants and shipmasters weep for all the loss of luxury and wealth (18:11–20). Finally, an angel throws a great millstone into the sea and says that Babylon will likewise be destroyed, bringing an end to its culture:

> "So will Babylon the great city be thrown down with violence, / and will be found no more; / and the sound of harpists and musicians, of flute players and trumpeters, / will be heard in you no more, / and a craftsman of any craft / will be found in you no more, / and the sound of the mill / will be heard in you no more, / and the light of a lamp / will shine in you no more, / and the voice of bridegroom and bride / will be heard in you no more, / for your merchants were the great ones of the earth, / and all nations were deceived by your sorcery. / And in her was found the blood of prophets and of saints, / and of all who have been slain on earth." (Rev. 18:21–24)

Note what Revelation describes here—wealth, music, and technology, accompanied by sorcery and murder. We are reading here of the end of the City of Cain just as it was described in Genesis 4 and understood by its ancient readers.

The City of God

The Bible's use of the same name for what happened with the tower at Babel, and for the empire called Babylon, is an anachronism. It is impossible to know exactly when the events depicted at the tower took place, but the empire known by this name flourished in the six and seventh centuries BC. The two are divided very likely by at least centuries if not millennia. If you connect all this with Eridu, which seems to have been founded around 5400 BC, it's clear that the Scriptures bring together multiple stories spanning a broad sweep of time. For our purposes, the dates don't really matter very much. The point is that the Babylon phenomenon is a narrative strand that begins with Cain and finds its fullness with the image of imperial Babylon. As we have seen, this whole complex of imagery goes into what we find in Revelation.

Notably, Revelation 18 also includes these words from the angel: "Come out of her, my people, / lest you take part in her sins, / lest you share in her plagues; / for her sins are heaped high as heaven, / and God has remembered her iniquities" (Rev. 18:4–5). Here is the call of God to those who would become His people: Come out of Babylon, because judgment is coming upon it. God does not merely call us out of Babylon, however. He provides a way out, and the narrative begins with Abraham, who lives in a place called Ur of the Chaldeans. *Ur* is a word that means simply "city," while the Chaldeans are of course the Babylonians—whose empire doesn't yet exist at the time of Abraham. Again, we are looking at the Bible anachronistically pulling in another story and setting it in Babylon.

Abraham's story, which you can read starting at the end of Genesis 11, immediately follows the Babel story, so the impression one gets is that God calls him out from Babel. The Ur that he left may be identified with a Sumerian city called Uruk, and it notably is the site of a great ziggurat, which you can visit in the modern country of Iraq. The Bible therefore presents a continuum of various names that all encompass one image, whether you want to call it Eridu, Babel, Ur, Uruk, or Babylon. This city is the creation of humans, filled with demonic evil and dominated by fallen angels who teach humans evil. God tasks Abraham, therefore, to leave Babylon and begin a new nation, which will become Israel, called out by God not only from Ur but eventually also from Egypt, which was functioning as Babylon for the Israelites in that period—a city of evil, ruled by demons.

Saint Augustine compares the wickedness of Babylon with the righteousness of the city of God:

> And certainly this is the great difference which distinguishes the two cities of which we speak, the one being the society of the godly men, the other of the ungodly, each associated with the angels that adhere to their party, and the one guided and fashioned by love of self, the other by love of God.[9]

Here, he refers not only to the radical difference in quality between God's godly civilization and humankind's ungodly one, but he also says that "each [are] associated with the angels that adhere to their party." That is, God's city is associated with obedient angels who lead humans toward salvation, while humankind's city is accompanied by demons, fallen angels who lead people away from God.

God's creation of Israel and then the final culmination of it as the New Jerusalem is the city St. Augustine is writing about. We see a glimpse of it in Revelation:

> The one who conquers, I will make him a pillar in the temple of my God. Never shall he go out of it, and I will write on him the name of my God, and the name of the city of my God, the new Jerusalem, which comes down from my God out of heaven, and my own new name. (Rev. 3:12)

---

9 Augustine of Hippo, *City of God*, trans. Marcus Dods, in *Nicene and Post-Nicene Fathers I*, ed. Philip Schaff, vol. 2 (Peabody, MA: Hendrickson Publishers, 1999), 273.

> Then I saw a new heaven and a new earth, for the first heaven and the first earth had passed away, and the sea was no more. And I saw the holy city, new Jerusalem, coming down out of heaven from God, prepared as a bride adorned for her husband. And I heard a loud voice from the throne saying, "Behold, the dwelling place of God is with man. He will dwell with them, and they will be his people, and God himself will be with them as their God. He will wipe away every tear from their eyes, and death shall be no more, neither shall there be mourning, nor crying, nor pain anymore, for the former things have passed away." (Rev. 21:1–4)

What characterizes the New Jerusalem, the City of God? Paradise, the restoration and fullness of Eden, the place where God dwells with humans and where humanity is joined to Him with joy in worship forever.

CHAPTER 6

The Worship of God

Then Moses and Aaron, Nadab, and Abihu, and seventy of the elders of Israel went up, and they saw the God of Israel. There was under his feet as it were a pavement of sapphire stone, like the very heaven for clearness. And he did not lay his hand on the chief men of the people of Israel; they beheld God, and ate and drank.

—Exodus 24:9–11

The work of the priesthood is done on earth, but it is ranked among heavenly ordinances. And this is only right, for no man, no angel, no archangel, no other created power, but the Paraclete himself ordained this succession, and persuaded men, while still remaining in the flesh to represent the ministry of angels. The priest, therefore, must be as pure as if he were standing in heaven itself, in the midst of those powers.

—St. John Chrysostom[1]

1 Saint John Chrysostom, *Six Books on the Priesthood* III.4, trans. Graham Neville (Crestwood, NY: St. Vladimir's Seminary Press, 2002), 70.

When the worship of God first appears in the Bible in Genesis 4, the text doesn't define what it is, nor do we get much detail about how people carried out that worship. There isn't even a recorded commandment from God that Cain and Abel were following. Fully detailed commands from God for how to worship Him don't appear until Leviticus, the third book of the Scriptures.

Nonetheless, people worshiped God over and over, prior to those detailed commands, and the worship is carried out not just by Adam and Eve's first sons but also by Noah, Abraham, Isaac, Jacob, and others. Likewise, we see pagans worshiping their gods. It's clear from the hints the Bible gives about worship in the pre-Leviticus texts that the worshipers know what they're doing. It's also clear that what they are doing—both the incipient Israel and the surrounding nations—is remarkably consistent even in comparison with each other. Worship was not an undefined action, and the original readers and hearers of Leviticus had worship experience before receiving those instructions. It doesn't come out of the blue with the giving of the Torah on Sinai.

So what exactly is worship in the historical Christian context? In contrast to the ancient world, in our modern period that question is not very easy to answer. Based on all the things that go by the name *worship* in English, it seems to mean "doing religious things," especially religious things directed toward God. So it might be singing songs or bowing, or it might be offering the Eucharist on an altar. *Worship* also gets used to refer to sermons or even socializing. Yet what did it mean for the ancient world in which Christianity arose? They seemed to know what it meant and how to do it.

Before we can see both the forest and the trees of this question, we need to clear out some linguistic underbrush for us English-speakers. In English, *worship* derives from *worth,* and for most of the history of *worship* in English, to worship someone or something is to ascribe worthiness, making it roughly a synonym of words like *praise* or *venerate*. Modern English retains this use of *worship* in only a few contexts. We might be familiar with the indirect address of British judges as "Your Worship" or the Anglican wedding service where the bride and groom say to each other "With my body I thee worship."

Translations of some religious texts also use *worship* this way, such as the January 16 feast in the Orthodox Church usually called "The Veneration of the Precious Chains of the Apostle Peter," but sometimes translated as "The *Worship* of the Precious Chains of the Apostle Peter." The festal texts even include hymns like this: "Without leaving Rome, thou didst come to us by the precious chains which thou didst wear, O foremost of the Apostles. And worshipping them with faith, we pray: By thine intercessions with God, grant us great mercy."[2] To those conditioned with the idea that worship is due to God alone, this language might seem shockingly idolatrous. Yet no one who calls a judge "Your Worship" or gets married using the *Book of Common Prayer* considers judges or newlyweds to be gods. Nor do Orthodox Christians who venerate the chains of St. Peter regard those chains as gods.

Given these examples and also the historical usage of *worship* in English, it's important to set aside the shock and ask this critical question: What are the *actions* this word is describing? If we ask that question and then look at those actions within the context of the ancient world in which human worship arose, then we can understand what Christian worship has historically meant and what it was understood to accomplish.

---

2 "Apolytikion of the Veneration of the Precious Chains of the Apostle Peter," in *The Menaion*, vol. 5, *The Month of January* (Brookline, MA: Holy Transfiguration Monastery, 2005), 146.

The House of God

The earliest known human settlements, in places such as Göbekli Tepe or Çatalhöyük, both in modern Turkey, or Jericho in the West Bank, all bear the marks of having been situated for cultic purposes—that is, they are worship centers. Still more, however, they show little or no indication of being located near natural resources or for strategic purposes. They are remote, illogical choices for human settlements, yet in some cases, massive buildings were constructed, no doubt at great expense of materials and labor. So why build worship centers in these places?

To understand what was going on here, let's look at Genesis 28, in which we see a visionary experience of Jacob, the grandson of Abraham:

> Jacob left Beersheba and went toward Haran.[3] And he came to a certain place and stayed there that night, because the sun had set. Taking one of the stones of the place, he put it under his head and lay down in that place to sleep. And he dreamed, and behold, there was a ladder [or *staircase*] set up on the earth, and the top of it reached to heaven. And behold, the angels of God were ascending and descending on it! And behold, the LORD stood above it and said, "I am the LORD, the God of Abraham your father and the God of Isaac. The land on which you lie I will give to you and to your offspring." (Gen. 28:10–13)

In this dream-vision, Jacob sees a staircase set on the earth and leading to heaven, often referred to as "Jacob's Ladder." The Hebrew word here is *sullām,* which the Scriptures use only in this one place, and it can be translated as either "ladder" or "staircase" because it refers not

---

3 The Haran this verse mentions might be in the same region in southeast Turkey where Göbekli Tepe is, though we have no reason to identify them as being the same place.

to a particular kind of object but rather to something on which one may walk up or down. Thus, Jacob sees God's angels going up and down on it. At the top he sees God Himself, who identifies Himself as the same God Abraham and Isaac knew.

What is Jacob's Ladder, exactly? Jacob tells us: "How awesome is this place! This is none other than the house of God, and this is the gate of heaven" (Gen. 28:17). *Gate of heaven* should ring a bell for us, given what we saw in the previous chapter with the Tower of Babel, whose Assyrian-origin name *Bab-ilu* means "gate of a god." While we might usually envision a ladder appearing in Genesis 28, it seems likely that what Jacob saw was in fact a ziggurat. Even if you don't accept the ziggurat identification, the biblical imagery does convey the idea that Jacob saw God in this place and identified it as a "gate" to the heavenly reality where one can access God and His angels. "Surely the Lord is in this place, and I did not know it," he says (Gen. 28:16). Here, Jacob saw and met God.

What he does next is critical:

> So early in the morning Jacob took the stone that he had put under his head and set it up for a pillar and poured oil on the top of it. He called the name of that place Bethel, but the name of the city was Luz at the first. Then Jacob made a vow, saying, "If God will be with me and will keep me in this way that I go, and will give me bread to eat and clothing to wear, so that I come again to my father's house in peace, then the Lord shall be my God, and this stone, which I have set up for a pillar, shall be God's house. And of all that you give me I will give a full tenth to you." (Gen. 28:18–22)

Jacob's response to his vision and his realization that "the Lord is in this place" is to set up a pillar and to consecrate it as belonging to the Lord by anointing it with oil. He also gives the place the name *Bethel*, which means "house of God." Further, he makes vows to God, especially that this particular place will be given to God and regarded as His house. It becomes a place of worship because of the visionary experience that Jacob had there, which revealed to him that God could be accessed there.

In pagan contexts, an encounter with a god was possible when the god was discovered to live in a particular place. While the Bible does not teach that God or the worship of God are confined by or limited to certain geographic places, nonetheless, the Scriptures do not negatively depict Jacob's setting aside of Bethel as a particular place for God. The Scriptures use the name afterward and even anachronistically many times before. If that is not enough, however, God Himself confirms this act by saying to Jacob later, "Arise, go up to Bethel and dwell there. Make an altar there to the God who appeared to you when you fled from your brother Esau" (Gen. 35:1).

This spiritual experience thus explains why ancient cultic centers sprung up in illogical places: someone had a vision in a place, and so people going on a pilgrimage began to return to the place and participate in that experience. In Jacob's case, he not only had the vision and designated the place as holy to God, but Genesis 35:7 puts his obedience to God's command into these very terms: "there he built an altar and called the place El-Bethel ["the God of Bethel"], because there God had revealed himself to him when he fled from his brother."

According to the Bible and also other sources, worship in the ancient world flowed out of experiences of the divine. It was not something ancient peoples invented within a mythos devised to explain natural phenomena. Places got set aside for worship because people said they met gods in those places.

What Is Worship For?

With some understanding of why particular places get used for worship, we therefore ask: Why is worship the response to such an experience? What do the worshipers hope to accomplish? If we set aside for a moment the religious category we have come to call *worship*, which tends to be bound up with a lot of technical considerations, and look at ancient people's actions when they worship their gods, we can get a sense of what they hoped to accomplish.

Consider the beginning of the worship relationship—a person encounters a divine being. What would that ancient person have thought when he or she met that spirit? If he or she met a demon, it may not have been a pleasant experience. The demon could have made it pleasant, though, as we know that even Satan can appear as an angel of light (2 Cor. 11:14). Either way, the human knows that he or she is encountering something powerful.

If you become aware that a powerful spiritual being lives near you, you could view that spirit as either a threat or an opportunity, or possibly both. What do you do when you hope to stave off a threat or make an ally? Even now, but most especially in the ancient world, you offer hospitality. Pagans offered hospitality to the demons they worshiped because they knew they were powerful and dangerous. Israel offered hospitality to God—and was offered hospitality *by* God—because of the relationship of mutual love. Worship as hospitality explains the whole complex of cultic behaviors we see in the ancient world—sacrifices, incense, poetry, hymns of praise, etc. The piece of this that might not make that much sense to us is sacrifice. How is that hospitality?[4]

We tend to think of sacrifice as being about giving something up or about killing. However, in the Levitical sacrifices that God commanded, and even from what we know of pagan sacrifices, the killing of animals was not ritualized, meaning that it was not considered

4 For a thorough treatment of this theme, see *Welcoming Gifts: Sacrifice in the Bible and Christian Life*, by Archimandrite Jeremy Davis (Ancient Faith Publishing, 2022).

critical to the sacrificial rite. Further, many sacrifices did not even involve animals—they also included drink, oil, grain, and cakes. In cultures farther afield, one can find sacrifices of fresh fruit, as well. What do these things all have in common? They are all food.

Incense is a sacrifice as well, though it is not consumed; rather, it renders foul air sweet or simply makes the air more pleasing, which is part of the larger sense of sacrifice as hospitality. We can see this kind of language in the Scriptures for incense (Lev. 2:2) and also for whole-burnt sacrifices, which is food that is wholly offered to God by means of burning (Ex. 29; Lev. 1).[5] The language emphasizes all this as a pleasing aroma to God. Some sacrifices were not whole-burnt sacrifices. Some portions would be set aside for the priests and the people making the offering, for eating, while some portions would be burnt. In this way, it was understood that worshipers were sharing a meal with their god. Across nearly every human culture throughout history, eating a meal together is the core, critical act of hospitality.

The full matrix of religious rituals ancient people practiced did not always include sacrifices of food or incense, but sacrifice was always the core of their relationship with their deities. Without the hospitality of sacrifice, there was no real relationship.

How Does Worship Work?

One of the most startling things one notices about worship in the ancient world is how much most ancient religions have in common with one another, even when comparing pagan worship with Israel's worship. If we remember, however, that everyone sought to share hospitality with their god, then this makes sense. From ancient

5 There are many references to this theme in the Scriptures when it talks about sacrifices. I am mentioning only a few here.

sources, including the Bible, we can see a typical outline of how sacrifice worked, particularly in the ancient Near East.[6]

The first step is the dedication of the elements to be sacrificed. In the context of Israel, a priest or elder might lay his hands upon an animal and say a prayer of offering (Lev. 4:15, 8:14–22). This dedication might be referred to as "sanctification," which simply means the setting apart of something for a purpose. Making something "holy" has the same meaning.

The next step is a procession with the sacrificial food to where it will be offered to the god, accompanied by hymns and prayers. If animals are to be sacrificed, they are typically slaughtered nearby. Notably, the slaughter is simply done in an efficient manner and is not ritualized, indicating that the killing itself is not what is important to the sacrifice. Animals were not made to suffer, and in some cases, a ritual offering of a tuft of their hair was placed into the censer, which was to indicate that the animal was considered to be going voluntarily.[7]

If an animal is being offered, its blood is drained and collected. Many pagan rituals included drinking blood or pouring out blood as an offering to the god, because it was understood, as it was in Israel, that "the life is in the blood" (Lev. 17:11–14), meaning that blood could be used to transfer power to the one who consumed it, a ritual predation. Pagans would also offer blood to dead heroes and spirits. For example, in *The Odyssey* by Homer, Odysseus does this

---

6 A thorough reading of both Exodus and Leviticus provides most of the details in the context of Israel. Walter Burkert discusses the pagan context in particular in *Homo Necans: The Anthropology of Ancient Greek Sacrificial Ritual and Myth* (Oakland, CA: University of California Press, 1986), as well as in some of his other works.

7 The Orthodox baptismal service includes the offering of hair, a first "sacrifice" to God given by the one about to be baptized. Some traditions likewise place this hair in the censer.

in hope that the ghost of the blind prophet Teiresias would answer his questions:

> When I had prayed sufficiently to the dead, I cut the throats of the two sheep and let the blood run into the trench, whereon the ghosts came trooping up from Erebus—brides, young bachelors, old men worn out with toil, maids who had been crossed in love, and brave men who had been killed in battle, with their armour still smirched with blood; they came from every quarter and flitted round the trench with a strange kind of screaming sound that made me turn pale with fear. When I saw them coming I told the men to be quick and flay the carcasses of the two dead sheep and make burnt offerings of them, and at the same time to repeat prayers to Hades and to Proserpine; but I sat where I was with my sword drawn and would not let the poor feckless ghosts come near the blood till Teiresias should have answered my questions.[8]

By contrast, God forbade His people to consume the blood (Lev. 17:10–14), though sacrificial blood was used for sprinkling in purification and atonement rituals (Lev. 4:5–18, 16:11–19).

The next step is to bring the sacrificial food to a table called the *prothesis*. There, portions are divided up. Depending on the ritual, some would be for the god, some for the priests, and some for the people making the sacrifice. If animals were being offered, they would be butchered at this point.

In the pagan context, the portion set aside for the gods was often the worst part, with the choicest reserved for the priests—while God commanded Israel to give to Him the best parts. The priest then took to the altar the portion offered to the god, where he touched it

8 Homer, *The Odyssey*, trans. Samuel Butler (Urbana, IL: Project Gutenberg, 1999), bk. XI, https://www.gutenberg.org/files/1727/1727-h/1727-h.htm.

and elevated it, lifting it up to the deity with many prayers. Then he burned it, the sweet smell rising up to the god. For pagans, the deity was present bodily in an idol, but Israel used no idols when worshiping Yahweh. Following the offering to the god, if there were portions reserved for the priests and for those who offered the sacrifice, they would then be taken to a ritual dining area and consumed along with many *trapezamata* ("table things"), which were side dishes for the feast. In the pagan context, drunkenness and sexual immorality were part of the feasts, but these were of course strictly forbidden to Israel.

This basic ritual order—dedication, procession, division of portions, lifting up to the deity, then ritual eating by priests and worshipers separately—is found in the Orthodox Christian Divine Liturgy to this very day. Does that mean that Orthodox worship is derived from paganism? Of course it doesn't mean that, any more than the worship of ancient Israel was derived from paganism. Both were commanded by God. So how are they different from paganism? The difference appears in the question of communion.

What Does Worship Do?

The eating of the sacrifices—and, for pagans, the immorality as well—put worshipers into communion with their god. What does it mean to be in communion with a god?

Sacrifices are hospitality, as I mentioned earlier, and coming together to eat and drink bind together those who share the table. They become one community. The guest receiving the hospitality becomes part of the household. Ancient people considered hospitality so sacred that violating it one way or the other—whether by host or guest—could bring a death penalty or some other curse upon the violator. This sacredness of hospitality is why, for instance, in Acts 14 the people of Lystra in central Anatolia (modern-day Turkey) attempt to sacrifice to Ss. Paul and Barnabas. After these apostles perform miracles of healing, the locals think them to be the Greek gods Hermes and Zeus—which of course the two apostles deny vehemently.

Why were the people of Lystra so eager to show them this divine hospitality? We can find the backstory in Ovid's *Metamorphoses,* which is set in Tyana, in the same region as Lystra. In the story, Zeus and Hermes make a visit disguised as peasants, and everyone refuses them hospitality but a poor couple named Baucis and Philemon. In revenge for the inhospitality, the two gods destroy the town with a flood but save the couple and transform their home into a temple. At death, the couple are transformed into intertwining trees that would live forever. Thus, the Lystrans did not want to suffer a similar fate as their forebears. The mythical tale also expresses what happens when people come into communion with a god. In such communion, the god shares his life with the community and the people become like the god. Baucis and Philemon do not become divine, but their life is transformed, even lasting into death.

Most sacrificial communion in the ancient world was far more prosaically designed, however. In the Greek pagan context, if you wanted to win in battle, you would worship Ares, the god of war. If you wanted to be successful in seduction, you might sacrifice to Aphrodite. If you sought wisdom, then you would worship Athena. If looking for agricultural success, you worshiped Demeter. Sacrifice was thus a kind of religious technology, and pagans understood this communion they performed through idolatry as manipulative—the god you served was almost forced to share itself with you.

The reality behind worshiping pagan gods is of course that the gods cannot actually deliver on their promises of strength and power. The Scriptures mention their weakness in numerous places, with perhaps one of the most famous demonstrations being how St. Elias proved that Baal the thunder god could not control the lightning (1 Kin. 18).

Even though the pagan gods are weak and powerless compared to Yahweh, worshiping them through sacrifices still puts the worshiper into communion with them. Saint Paul identifies this as communion with demons (1 Cor. 10:20–21). This communion transforms the worshiper to become like the demons they worship. If one looks at the behavior of the gods of the pagans, who are violent, promiscuous, rapacious, avaricious, gluttonous, and so forth—according to the pagans' own accounts of their gods—then one can understand the vicious cruelty and inhumanity of the ancient pagan world.[9]

Understanding all this, then, we can see how sacrificing to Yahweh, the God of Israel—which puts worshipers into communion with Him—is supremely beneficial. If you become like what you worship, then bringing God into your community and being brought into His makes you like Him. What is God like? He is not only unlike the pagan gods in terms of their immorality, but He is also supremely powerful and capable. Communion with God is why the saints are righteous and can perform mighty works in the name of Christ.

Fundamentally, then, in terms of its basic actions, worship is not different between pagans and God's people. What made it different was who was at the table of hospitality with them. Pagans invited the likes of Zeus, Thor, and so on to their tables, and their societies became like these gods. Israel invited the loving Creator of all to the table, and thus they became like Him.

The Eucharist

When Christ offered the Eucharist to His disciples in the Gospels, He commanded them to "do this as my remembrance" (Luke 22:14–20; 1 Cor. 11:24–25). It may not be obvious to us that He is giving the Eucharist as a sacrifice according to the pattern we just discussed above, but a look at the Old Testament shows that a "remembrance"

---

9 For a thorough telling of the moral state of ancient pagan society, see Tom Holland's *Dominion: How the Christian Revolution Remade the World* (New York: Basic Books, 2021).

or "memorial" before God was about offering sacrifice (Lev. 2:2–16, 5:12, 6:15, 24:7, etc.). Thus, this was Jesus telling His disciples how to worship Him, and just like it had always been, the core ritual act is the shared meal offered to God. Jesus' command here is to offer up bread and wine, which He says are to be His Body and Blood (Matt. 26:26–28; Mark 14:22–25; Luke 22:14–20).

Eating what has been offered to God is life-giving, as Jesus Himself said:

> "Truly, truly, I say to you, unless you eat the flesh of the Son of Man and drink his blood, you have no life in you. Whoever feeds on my flesh and drinks my blood has eternal life, and I will raise him up on the last day. For my flesh is true food, and my blood is true drink. Whoever feeds on my flesh and drinks my blood abides in me, and I in him. As the living Father sent me, and I live because of the Father, so whoever feeds on me, he also will live because of me. This is the bread that came down from heaven, not like the bread the fathers ate, and died. Whoever feeds on this bread will live forever." (John 6:53–58)

Communion with the God who created us and loves us thus gives immortality, resurrection to life everlasting. Without that communion, "you have no life in you."

When Christ gave the Eucharist, He made many important distinctions—which the Orthodox Church practices even today—that set it apart from the sacrifices of ancient Israel and of paganism. The most important of them largely resolve into "where" (in a sense) Christ appears in the sacrifice. Christ is the one "that offereth and is offered, that accepteth and is distributed."[10]

One continuity is that the deity is still the one who accepts the sacrifice, with Christ as He "that accepteth." Yet a major discontinuity

10 Prayer of the Cherubic Hymn, *Divine Liturgy of St. John Chrysostom*.

is in the offerer: no longer does a human priest make the offering, but Christ Himself is "He that offereth." The bishop or presbyter at the altar participates in Christ's priesthood and is thus considered a priest, but he is not *of himself* considered a priest.

Another discontinuity is in what is being offered. Rather than animals or cakes, Christ Himself is the one who "is offered." He provides Himself for us, offering *us* His own hospitality, giving even Himself to be the one distributed—the greatest possible offering that could be made. Instead of humans feeding their gods in exchange for favors, the God-man Himself feeds us and needs nothing from us, giving Himself out of love.

For these reasons, the core action of worship in the Orthodox Church—the sacrificial meal of Christ's own Body and Blood—is called the *Eucharist,* from the Greek *eucharistia,* meaning "thanksgiving." We offer thanksgiving to God in response to this profound, mystical, life-giving hospitality He offers to us. We have become the guests. He has made us part of His own household. God has flipped the plot, so to speak, and shown what all those sacrifices of the ancient world always pointed to—that God has invited us to His own table and is giving us nothing less than Himself.

CHAPTER 7

War Against the Gods

For I will pass through the land of Egypt that night, and I will strike all the firstborn in the land of Egypt, both man and beast; and on all the gods of Egypt I will execute judgments: I am the Lord.

—Exodus 12:12

The saint said, "My parents call me Alban and I shall ever adore and worship the true and living God who created all things." The judge answered very angrily, "If you wish to enjoy the happiness of everlasting life, you must sacrifice at once to the mighty gods." Alban answered, "The sacrifices which you offer to devils cannot help their votaries nor fulfil the desires and petitions of their suppliants. On the contrary, he who has offered sacrifices to these images will receive eternal punishment in hell as his reward."

—St. Bede the Venerable[1]

1 Bede, *The Ecclesiastical History of the English People* 1.7, eds. Judith McClure and Roger Collins (Oxford: Oxford University Press, 1999), 17.

PERHAPS ONE OF THE MOST unappreciated aspects of the Scripture and of the rest of the Orthodox Tradition is how much of it was formulated precisely as a response to paganism. In the pages of Scripture, we find not only apologetics against paganism but also corrections of pagan accounts of the world, appropriations of pagan imagery and language, and even satirical hurling of insults.

I've already discussed a number of specific responses to paganism in the preceding chapters. In this one we will consider a more theoretical approach to paganism according to what we see in Scripture and also look at some of the particular gods who formed part of the spiritual "neighborhood" of Israel and whom sinful leaders often invited into Israel. Israel generally addressed paganism with three possible responses—syncretism, direct opposition, or co-opting elements of paganism for Yahweh. I will incorporate discussion of these three as this chapter proceeds.

Myth and Mythology

I've used the words *myth, mythic,* and *mythology* many times in this book, but now it's time to define them a little more precisely as we consider a more theoretical approach to paganism. In its basic sense, *myth* (from Greek *mythos*) means "story." I've used *mythic* a number of times in this book to refer to this sense of story, but of course I am talking about the kinds of stories that are usually called "myths"—stories involving interaction between the seen and unseen world. In popular usage, we tend to use *myth* to mean a story that is not true, but that is not its original sense, and certainly the ancient people for whom myths were part of their religion did not think of them that way. *Myth* also does not get used that way in the technical sense in the study of history and religion.

The academic discipline of ritual theory makes a useful distinction between *myth* and *mythology.* A myth is a story people participate in through rituals that not only make the story part of their lives and shape their imaginations, but they are also the means through which participants enter into the story themselves. The ancient Greek myth of Persephone's abduction by Hades, for instance, was not only a story that Greek pagans told but one in which they participated by engaging in a ritual search for the abducted goddess, seeking her out and not finding her, joining themselves to the search by her goddess mother Demeter in the process.[2] Christians also of course participate in the myths of Christianity through many kinds of rituals, most memorably in Holy Week, when we participate in the stories of the life of Christ, and at Pascha, participating in both Christ's Resurrection and the Passover and Exodus from Egypt.

Myth, then, contrasts with *mythology,* which are the stories leftover when the ritual participation has fallen into disuse. There is a connection here with the popular use of *myth* as an untrue story, but it may not be obvious at first. We tend to think that people stop participating in religious rituals because they don't believe in the related stories anymore, but in my pastoral ministry and experience, I have observed that the opposite is usually true. More often, belief falls away after participation falls away, showing that conviction flows from conditioning. It is the ritual participation in the story that plants it firmly within the human person. Why do most people regard the ancient pagan myths as fanciful, untrue stories? Not because they have made a careful investigation into the stories as truth claims, but rather because they no longer have the experience of being joined to the story through ritual.

I will not go into it here, but given this reality, it is interesting at least to raise the question of what happens to Christians when Christianity is de-ritualized. When people stop ritually participating in

2 You can read about these rituals in some detail in *Finding Persephone: Women's Rituals in the Ancient Mediterranean,* eds. Maryline Parca and Angeliki Tzanetou (Bloomington, IN: Indiana University Press, 2007).

the stories of Christianity, does the Christian myth turn into mere mythology for them? Or what if the rituals change, and the participation is in another kind of story?

Pro-Demon Propaganda

Given what I just said, it's worth noting that nowhere in the Old Testament do we see a command from God about not *believing* in pagan stories. Why? Because no one thought of religion that way at the time. Belief was not focused on what one *agreed* was true or, still less, on how one *felt* about religious matters. Rather, God's commands about the pagan religious traditions surrounding Israel are of this type:

> "You shall have no other gods before me. You shall not make for yourself a carved image, or any likeness of anything that is in heaven above, or that is in the earth beneath, or that is in the water under the earth. You shall not bow down to them or serve them, for I the LORD your God am a jealous God, visiting the iniquity of the fathers on the children to the third and the fourth generation of those who hate me, but showing steadfast love to thousands of those who love me and keep my commandments." (Ex. 20:3–6)

The command is very clear—do not make idols of gods, bowing before them and serving them. To "serve" a god is to engage in the worship I described in the previous chapter, but it is not only to offer up sacrifices but to enter into the whole matrix of rituals involved in the myths of pagan gods. Why? Because God "is a jealous God," meaning that He has set aside Israel for Himself and will not share them. The command not to participate in the rituals of the pagan gods gets repeated numerous times throughout the Scriptures. More than anything else, worshiping only Yahweh the God of Israel—and no other—was what made His people different from the people of all the other nations.

So, apart from the actual worship of the gods of the nations, how were pagan *stories* to be understood? Obviously, God's faithful people in the Scriptures did not actually *believe* stories such as how Zeus overthrew his father Chronos and set himself up as the most high god. Nor did they teach that it was true that Baal did something similar by defeating Yam and Nahar and setting up his own father El as most high god, with himself as the leader of the divine council. Both of these stories are based on something that the Bible says is true—there was a prominent divine being who attempted to overthrow the Most High God. The Scriptures, however, identify that rebellious spirit as the devil, not as the object of worship. Moreover, instead of being victorious, the rebel is defeated and thrown down from the divine council (Is. 14:12–21; Ez. 28:11–19).

Since we know from God's revelation what the *true* story is, we can see that the pagan accounts are essentially pro-demon propaganda. Like most propaganda, they are based on something true, but they are given a spin that is to the demons' advantage, for the purpose of getting humans to worship them and join them in their destruction. The way demons treat humans is not so much for their own benefit—how can one benefit a demon? Rather, it is for the detriment of humans. Having lost the war against God, being incapable of actually taking His place, demons seek revenge by drawing humanity into evil and therefore destruction and damnation.

As we can see, the way the people of God responded to these stories, both before and after the coming of Christ, was not simply to deny that they were true but rather to identify what in them was useful, and in many cases offer correction. Since Israel and the Church did not participate in the rituals related to these stories, they had moved from *myth* to *mythology* for them, bereft of the sting of demonic communion. Reading a story isn't what puts you into communion with demons and makes you like them, but rather engaging in ritual worship of them and also in doing the work of demons—sin (Ps. 115:4–8; John 8:44).

Saint Basil's Bees

Many people in our own day look at these stories from paganism and balk at the idea that Christians might read them. Some extend this hesitation forward to any stories that include tales of spirits, heroes, gods, and monsters—this might include modern fantasy novels. As we've seen, though, the Bible itself includes stories like these, and as I will show further on, the biblical text sometimes takes elements from pagan stories and reclaims them for God.

But even if we do not worship the pagan gods, aren't paganism's stories hopelessly corrupt? Aren't they dangerous for Christians to read? To answer that question, let's turn to one of the greatest theologians of the early Church, a man who lived at a time when paganism was still present and part of the dominant culture, even though it was on the wane—St. Basil the Great.

Saint Basil (AD 330–379) was the bishop of Caesarea in Cappadocia in what is modern-day Turkey, and there were plenty of pagans still around at the time. As part of his teaching office as a bishop, he wrote a text commonly titled "An Address to Young Men on the Right Use of Greek Literature." The "young men" were students (most students at the time were male), and the "Greek" literature was of course the pagan mythology found in works such as those written by Homer and Hesiod. Here St. Basil sets out his basic theory for reading these texts:

> To begin with the poets, since their writings are of all degrees of excellence, you should not study all of their poems without omitting a single word. When they recount the words and deeds of good men,

> you should both love and imitate them, earnestly emulating such conduct. But when they portray base conduct, you must flee from them and stop up your ears, as Odysseus is said to have fled past the song of the sirens, for familiarity with evil writings paves the way for evil deeds. Therefore the soul must be guarded with great care, lest through our love for letters it receive some contamination unawares, as men drink in poison with honey.[3]

Saint Basil does not say "Never read this stuff!" Rather, he says to read critically. If you find something good, praise it and imitate it. If you find something bad, neither praise it nor imitate it. Fascinatingly, in the course of this exhortation, he actually does what he says to do, using a scene from Homer's *Odyssey* as an illustration. We saw earlier how Odysseus poured out blood for dead spirits—not something any Christian should imitate—but here he avoids the song of the sirens, just as Christians ought to avoid giving their rapt attention to evil in tales.

The saint goes on to address the evil of the pagan gods, which readers will find in their stories:

> We shall not praise the poets when they scoff and rail, when they represent fornicators and winebibbers, when they define blissfulness by groaning tables and wanton songs. Least of all shall we listen to them when they tell us of their gods, and especially when they represent them as being many, and not at one among themselves. For, among these gods, at one time brother is at variance with brother, or the father with his children; at another, the children

3 Saint Basil, "Address to Young Men on the Right Use of Greek Literature," in *Essays on the Study and Use of Poetry by Plutarch and Basil the Great,* ed. Frederick Morgan Padelford (New York: H. Holt and Company, 1902), IV, https://www.tertullian.org/fathers/basil_litterature01.htm.

> engage in truceless war against their parents. The adulteries of the gods and their amours, and especially those of the one whom they call Zeus, chief of all and most high, things of which one cannot speak, even in connection with brutes, without blushing, we shall leave to the stage.

What does he mean by saying that we should not "listen to them"? Taken out of context, one might interpret this to mean that Christians should not read or listen to these stories at all, but that would go against everything else he says in the text. It would also make him a hypocrite because he obviously has enough knowledge of pagan literature to make numerous allusions to it in the address. What this means is rather that we should not pay heed to the glory that the pagan authors give to the gods and other sinners in their stories, and again, we should not imitate their behavior; we should leave it "to the stage," i.e., to the theatres where one might encounter the stories.

Saint Basil's overall theory for reading pagan literature finds its summary in this famous passage:

> Now, then, altogether after the manner of bees must we use these writings, for the bees do not visit all the flowers without discrimination, nor indeed do they seek to carry away entire those upon which they light, but rather, having taken so much as is adapted to their needs, they let the rest go. So we, if wise, shall take from heathen books whatever befits us and is allied to the truth, and shall pass over the rest. And just as in culling roses we avoid the thorns, from such writings as these we will gather everything useful, and guard against the noxious. So, from the very beginning, we must examine each of their teachings, to harmonize it with our ultimate purpose, according to the Doric proverb, "testing each stone by the measuring-line."

From this and the previous passages, we can see that St. Basil's advice about this literature takes three basic forms: read only what is high quality, take away and imitate the good, avoid and do not imitate the bad. Here, he even quotes a Doric proverb, which likely arises in a pagan context—again putting into practice the very advice he gives.

What St. Basil says applies even outside the question of reading pagan literature or other texts that have such elements in them. We can treat whatever we encounter in life with the virtues of the bee, taking what is good and leaving behind the bad. One does not even have to engage in constant apologetics against the bad. One can simply leave it alone.

The universal applicability of St. Basil's method of interpretation is why he makes what might seem like a shocking statement:

> Into the life eternal the Holy Scriptures lead us, which teach us through divine words. But so long as our immaturity forbids our understanding their deep thought, we exercise our spiritual perceptions upon profane writings, which are not altogether different, and in which we perceive the truth as it were in shadows and in mirrors. Thus we imitate those who perform the exercises of military practice, for they acquire skill in gymnastics and in dancing, and then in battle reap the reward of their training. We must needs believe that the greatest of all battles lies before us, in preparation for which we must do and suffer all things to gain power. Consequently we must be conversant with poets, with historians, with orators, indeed with all men who may further our soul's salvation. Just as dyers prepare the cloth before they apply the dye, be it purple or any other color, so indeed must we also, if we would preserve indelible the idea of the true virtue, become first initiated in the pagan lore, then at length give special heed to the sacred and divine teachings, even as we first accustom

> ourselves to the sun's reflection in the water, and then become able to turn our eyes upon the very sun itself.[4]

He actually says here that we must "become first initiated in the pagan lore, then at length give special heed to the sacred and divine teachings"—learn the pagan texts *before* turning to the Bible. Why? Because we acquire the basic skills we need for reading and interpretation with this lesser literature before we can understand the deeper things of the Bible, the "shadows" and "reflection" we apprehend before we can gaze upon the sun. Thus, far from telling Christians to avoid anything that does not have a Christian label on it, St. Basil says that "we must be conversant with poets, with historians, with orators, indeed with all men who may further our soul's salvation"—that includes even pagans.

Before we turn to some specifics related to paganism in the Bible, I will say one last thing here in terms of our theoretical approach. If the stories of paganism really are "pro-demon propaganda," why does St. Basil find so much that is useful in them?

On the one hand, one might say it is because the demons behind paganism can't afford to let everything about their religion be a lie. After all, some of it would have to be attractive to ordinary people. What seems to me more likely, is that since these stories are in the hands of humans and we can see they have variation across time and space, it is the goodness of the human as created by God that is at work in them. Saint Justin Martyr in the second century makes this same argument, saying that these truths come via the prophets:

> For Moses is more ancient than all the Greek writers. And whatever both philosophers and poets have said concerning the immortality of

4 Saint Basil, "Address," II.

> the soul, or punishments after death, or contemplation of things heavenly, or doctrines of the like kind, they have received such suggestions from the prophets as have enabled them to understand and interpret these things. And hence there seem to be seeds of truth [*spermatikos logos*] among all men; but they are charged with not accurately understanding [the truth] when they assert contradictories.[5]

Thus, not everything in a story told by a human storyteller will be altogether evil, and indeed, since humanity was made for virtue, humans will put virtue forward in their stories, sometimes because of what they pick up from better sources. In this process, then, what demons have meant for evil, God, through human agency, has turned to good (see Gen. 50:20).

Baal

Here I want to spend a little time looking at some of the gods the Old Testament mentions, the pagan deities of the ancient Near East.[6] This context should be helpful when we read the Scriptures, and it will help us to recognize when the Scriptures directly address these religious traditions.

The most prominent among the pagan gods mentioned in the Scriptures is Baal (or *Ba'al*).[7] The word *ba'al* by itself simply means "lord" or "owner," so it does not necessarily refer to a deity, yet the Old Testament uses it this way in ninety places to refer to one of

---

5 Saint Justin Martyr, *First Apology,* in *Ante-Nicene Fathers,* trans. and eds. Alexander Roberts, James Donaldson, and A. Cleveland Coxe, vol. 1 (Peabody, MA: Hendrickson Publishers, 1999), 177.

6 In the next chapter, I will deal with Indo-European paganism, which includes the Greek paganism which is more visible in the New Testament.

7 The form *Baal* (without the apostrophe) is a transliteration from the Greek Septuagint and is repeated in the Latin Vulgate.

the gods of Canaanite paganism.[8] He is called *Baal-Hadad* in some ancient sources.

Why do the Scriptures mention him so often? He is not only the primary god the Canaanites worship (the people present in and near the land of ancient Israel), but the Israelites themselves also worship him at various times. Perhaps most famously, after the Northern Kingdom of Israel splits from Judah in the south, Baal worship takes over the royal family, particularly when King Ahab's wife Jezebel brings in prophets and priests of Baal while she is persecuting those who are faithful to Yahweh. *Jezebel* itself is a theophoric, a name including the name of a god, with the ending *-bel* being a reference to her god Baal.

Canaanite mythology depicts Baal as the son of the most high god El (a Semitic word that means *god*). He is a thunder god, associated with fertility through the rain but also with procreation and livestock, which is why bull imagery is connected with him. The worship of Baal included not only the usual sacrifices given to gods everywhere in the ancient Near East but also unspeakable acts such as bestiality. In the associated mythology, Baal and his father defeat Yam (the god of the ocean) and his son Nahar (the river god), deposing them and taking their places as most high god and ruler over the divine council, respectively. Baal also famously faces off against Mot, the Canaanite god of death, who kills him. Mot in turn gets killed by Anat, Baal's wife (and sister), paving the way for Baal to return triumphantly from the underworld. These stories, along with other mythological stories of the Canaanite religion, appear in the *Baal Cycle,* a series of poems in the ancient Semitic language Ugaritic preserved on clay tablets that identify Baal with the god Hadad (thus, the occasional form *Baal-Hadad*). These tablets date from around 1300–1500

---

8 For more detail on Baal, see *Dictionary of Deities and Demons in the Bible,* eds. Karel van der Toorn, Bob Becking, and Pieter W. van der Hoorst (Boston: Brill, 1999), 132ff.

BC and were lost with the destruction in 1185 BC of the city of Ugarit, located in northern Syria. They were unearthed in 1928.

The most famous incident regarding Baal in the Scriptures is when Yahweh defeats him through the prophet Elijah on Mount Carmel in 1 Kings 18. In this face-off with the prophets of Baal, St. Elijah shows that it is Yahweh who controls the rain, first when He stops it in the previous chapter (1 Kin. 17:1) and then by bringing it again, along with lightning from the sky. It is not only Yahweh's show of power that inspires the people to say "[Yahweh] is God" (1 Kin. 18:39) but specifically that this power in particular is shown not to belong to Baal. No matter how much Baal's prophets call out to him to send the lightning and rain, they demonstrate only the adage from the Psalms that "the gods of the nations are worthless [*'elilim*]" (Ps. 96:5 NET).

Less well-known is that there are elements of Scripture that draw directly on Baal imagery to show Christ's glory and victory. For instance, Baal as storm god is called "rider on the clouds" in the *Baal Cycle,* imagery that was taken over for the enthronement scene where the Son of Man comes on the clouds of heaven in Daniel 7:13 and Mark 14:62. The Scriptures use this language not to say that Baal is really the Son of God but that Baal has stolen imagery that really belongs to Christ. Further, Psalm 24 draws upon the narrative of the *Baal Cycle.* In the myth, Baal ascends Mount Zaphon to take control of the council of the gods. As he is announcing that he will defeat Yam and Nahar, messengers from those gods arrive and warn the assembled gods not to side with Baal. In a show of humility, the gods put their heads between their knees. Baal rebukes them, saying, "Lift up your heads, O gods!"

Psalm 24 responds to this myth by saying that the whole world belongs to God and He has "founded it upon the seas [*yam*] / and established it upon the rivers [*nahar*]" (Ps. 24:2), an image not of God doing battle with Yam and Nahar but essentially dropping the earth on top of them. Further, the psalm asks "Who shall ascend the hill of the Lord? / And who shall stand in his holy place?" (Ps. 24:3). Not the corrupt, evil Baal, but rather "He who has clean hands and a pure heart," that is, the Son of God, the true ruler of the divine council (Ps. 24:4). Finally, the last verses of the psalm declare "Lift up your heads, O gates," warning that the King of Glory is entering (Ps. 24:7–10). For many centuries, the Orthodox Church has used these words to depict Christ's invasion of the underworld, both in the fourth-century *Gospel of Nicodemus* and also ritually at the Paschal services while the priest bangs on the door with the cross. How does this relate to Baal's story?

In the *Cycle*, Kothar-wa-Khasis builds Baal's palace with its base in the underworld. When Christ stands at the doors of Hades and these words from the psalm are spoken, Baal is not only identified with the devil but has his own words thrown insultingly in his face. Thus, even though the stories of the *Cycle* were lost for over three thousand years, the Orthodox Church preserved the understanding of what the psalm meant in terms of Christ's place as the ruler of the divine council and the victor over death.

Marduk

Several other deities make significant appearances in the Old Testament, and these are all part of the "spiritual neighborhood" (if I may) of ancient Israel. Probably the most important of these is Marduk, the god of the city of Babylon. Like Baal, he is associated with bulls, and he is often accompanied in imagery with a dragon, a creature whom he defeated and tamed. By the time of the Neo-Babylonian Empire depicted in the Scriptures, Marduk is worshiped as the supreme god of the pantheon. The Scriptures not only mention Marduk's name directly, but his name appears in 2 Kings 20:12 and Isaiah 39:1, which include the theophoric name of the Babylonian king Marduk-apla-iddina II ("Marduk has given a son," in the Bible, *Merodach-baladan*).

There is also a story involving Marduk found in Daniel 14:1–22, which is only in Greek-tradition Old Testaments, in a section commonly referred to as Bel and the Dragon. The story takes place during the Babylonian captivity of Israel. *Bel,* here, is simply a transliteration of *Baal,* but the word does not refer necessarily to the Canaanite Baal. As noted above, *baal* means "lord," so this term can apply to any deity or even human masters, but it does seem that the Bel worshiped in Babylon at this time was an assimilation of Marduk along with the Canaanite Baal, as well as the Mesopotamian gods Enlil and Dumuzid.

By this point in Babylonian history (sixth-century BC), the Persian king Cyrus the Great had conquered Babylon. Cyrus himself is involved in the story, worshiping Marduk even though he is not a Babylonian. Why? In ancient paganism, although pagan kingdoms fought against each other, they generally did not say that other pagans' deities did not exist. Rather, they regarded the other gods as allies of their enemies. Cyrus thus comes to worship Marduk because he wants the god to be on his side and not to stir up the Babylonians in rebellion against him. In this story, an idol of Marduk was believed to consume large amounts of food every night. By sprinkling ashes on the floor that revealed footprints the next morning, the prophet Daniel proved that it was in fact Baal's priests who sneaked into the sealed chamber of the idol and ate sumptuously along with their families. The story shows the futility of idolatry, that the gods worshiped in the idols were not even capable of eating the food pagans offered to them.

Sources outside the Bible corroborate this account. The fifth-century BC Greek historian Herodotus mentions a great ziggurat in Babylon that modern historians have identified with Etemenanki, an archaeological site about sixty miles south of Baghdad in Iraq. Herodotus refers to the ziggurat as dedicated to "Zeus Belus," an indication that he believed the god worshiped there to be the same god as Zeus. Near the ziggurat was a place called Esagila, a temple dedicated to Marduk that included an idol of the god. Etemenanki has been associated with the Tower of Babel. With the Bible's conflation of the Babel events with Babylon (remember that the names are the same in Hebrew) and the Abraham story immediately following, the overall narrative is that God calls Abraham out of a world that was dedicated to the worship of Marduk.

Asherah

A few more deities are worth mentioning here. Included in the Canaanite pantheon is the goddess Asherah, who is variously the consort of El or his son Baal. The Old Testament mentions her nineteen times, often in association with trees or wooden poles, which were used as part of her cult. Although *Asherah* is the name of a goddess, the term refers to sacred trees and poles (made of wood or stone) used in idolatry, so we should not understand every reference to asherah in the Bible as about this goddess in particular. God commanded many times that these cultic objects be cut down and destroyed, as Israel syncretized idolatry into its life many times (Deut. 16:21; Judg. 6:25–30). Solomon himself worshiped Asherah (2 Kin. 23:13–14), but finally the righteous king Hezekiah opposed this idolatry (2 Kin. 18:4), though Manasseh later restored it (2 Kin. 21:2–9), and the righteous Josiah again destroyed it (2 Kin. 23:4–14).

Given this background of syncretistic Asherah worship in Israel, it should be no surprise that a certain eighth-century pottery fragment found in northern Sinai includes the phrase "Yahweh and his asherah." Some scholars have spun this inscription out into a narrative in which Israel was originally polytheistic and only later shed the various gods and goddesses in favor of worshiping Yahweh alone. They also say that Yahweh originally had a wife who got edited out of the Bible, and that the biblical narrative is covering up polytheism in favor of later monotheists who found it embarrassing. This identification has a major linguistic problem, however. The instance of *asherah* on that inscription is in a grammatical declension of the noun that texts never used for the goddess by that name. That means asherah here can only refer to the ritual pole, a tree, or possibly a grove. It was, in any event, an idolatrous object. It is likely that Israel did, at points, worship Yahweh using the ritual object known as an asherah, which is idolatrous behavior (like the worship of Yahweh via the golden calves).

We should not be surprised by that, though, because the Old Testament demonstrates that Israel fell into idolatry many times. At the same time, God was telling them to stop it. The biblical text does not cover up Israel's idolatrous polytheism at all. Rather, the text exposes and condemns it, and praises rulers who opposed it. In any event, neither the biblical text nor archaeological finds show that Yahweh actually had a wife—neither Asherah nor anyone else.

Other Idols in and near Israel

Asherah is only one of many gods that Israel worshiped idolatrously, both during the period of rule by judges and also by the kings of both the united and divided Israel. We mentioned Baal earlier, but Solomon also built shrines for Shemesh, a Canaanite sun god, which included horses and chariots (1 Kin. 11:7; 2 Kin. 23:11). He is also called *Chemosh* or *Kamosh*. Shemesh—whose name means simply "sun"—was worshiped in Jerusalem before King David conquered the city (2 Sam. 5). The fact that three different places in Israel were named for him attests to this worship—*Beth Shemesh* ("House [Temple] of Shemesh"), En-Shemesh, and Ir-Shemesh. The Moabites worshiped him,[9] and the name *Samson* derives from this god.

The local version of Shemesh worshiped in Jerusalem prior to David's conquest was called Shemesh-Tzedakah. The epithet *tzedek* shows up in the theophoric name *Melchizedek* ("my king is Tzedek"),

9 Judges 11:24–28 also identifies him as the god of the Ammonites.

which belonged to a priest-king of Jerusalem who worshiped Yahweh (Gen. 14:18–20) yet apparently had pagan parents who named him. The title *Shemesh-Tzedakah* ("sun of righteousness") gets appropriated for Christ in Malachi 4:2, and it appears in numerous hymns of the Orthodox Church.

Other gods that the Israel of the Old Testament worshiped include the Canaanite Astarte (Ashtoreth, Ishtar) and the Moabites' Milkom. Solomon also introduced the worship of Molech (or Moloch) into Israel (1 Kin. 11:7), a particularly egregious and evil cult that burned children in sacrifice to the demon. Israel does not seem to have worshiped the Philistines' fish god Dagon (or Dagan), but he figures into the Samson story, when Samson destroys Dagon's temple and kills himself in the process (Judg. 16:23). Dagon also appears in 1 Samuel 5, when the Philistines capture the Ark of the Covenant and bring it into their temple, where Dagon's idol falls down before it.

Spiritual Warfare

Given the presence of all this idolatry in and surrounding ancient Israel, we can understand why the Scriptures mention it so often. The Bible does not describe this idolatry as merely a distraction but rather as abomination, as betrayal of Yahweh their God, who said to them from the beginning that He is a jealous God. For this reason, St. Joshua said to the people of Israel at the renewal of the covenant at Shechem:

> Now therefore fear the Lord and serve him in sincerity and in faithfulness. Put away the gods that your fathers served beyond the River and in Egypt, and serve the Lord. And if it is evil in your eyes to serve the Lord, choose this day whom you will serve, whether the gods your fathers served in the region beyond the River, or the gods of the Amorites in whose land you dwell. But as for me and my house, we will serve the Lord. (Josh. 24:14–15)

The overarching narrative of Israel's journey in the Old Testament is about whether they will serve Yahweh or other gods. In far too many cases, it was the latter.

The gods of these pagan nations are fallen angelic beings, rebels who turned away from God. Their primary sin was seeking to turn the worship of humans away from God and toward themselves. Although God had created them in love to worship and serve Him, which also meant they would lead humankind to do the same, they rebelled and fell, becoming His enemies. Spiritual warfare therefore consists primarily of God making war against these demonic enemies, opposing them and rendering judgment against them (Ex. 12:12; Ps. 82:1–7). God judges the fallen gods not only to punish them but rather to put things right, and this consists primarily of dethroning these gods and rescuing humankind from their malevolent influence, because they have been leading humanity into sin and destruction.

The New Testament includes these themes of spiritual warfare, as well, as the Virgin Mary prophesied that in becoming incarnate, God "has brought down the mighty from their thrones" (Luke 1:52). Spiritual warfare is the very reason that Christ came into this world: "The reason the Son of God appeared was to destroy the works of the devil" (1 John 3:8).

So how do Christians participate in this warfare? We ourselves are called to wrestle "against the rulers, against the authorities, against the cosmic powers over this present darkness, against the spiritual forces of evil in the heavenly places" (Eph. 6:12), so how do we do that? We do it precisely by doing the works of God, by being faithful, by being true sons and daughters of our Father in heaven. Sometimes people think that spiritual warfare consists of a specialized kind of prayer or discipline called "exorcism," and of course the Church has particular prayers of exorcism, especially those prayed at the beginning of a baptism, which includes passages like this:

> The Lord who came into the world and dwelt among men rebuketh thee, O devil, that he might bring down thy tyranny and raise up mankind; he who upon the tree did triumph over the adversarial powers when the sun was darkened, the earth was being shaken, the graves were being opened and the bodies of the saints were arising; he who dissolved death by death and made powerless him who exercised the dominion over death; that is, thee, the devil. I adjure thee by God who showed forth the tree of life and who posted the cherubim and the flaming sword turning every way to guard it. Be rebuked and depart! For I adjure thee by that One who walked upon the surface of the sea as on dry land and rebuked the stormy winds, whose glance drieth up the abysses and whose threatening melteth the mountains; for he himself commandeth thee, even now, through us. Be afraid, come out, withdraw from this creature and do not return again.[10]

These prayers are a major part of the life of the Church, but they are only part of a whole matrix of exorcistic living.

Even if he or she does not consciously worship demons, every sinful thing a person does puts him or her into union with demonic forces. Likewise, whenever he or she does a work that belongs to God—not just "good deeds" or "religious acts" like prayer or fasting but every creative act of beauty, order, love, humility, kindness, and justice—it puts him or her into union with God. Every good thing we do is a pledge or renewal of allegiance to Yahweh our God. We may therefore understand the life of Christian faithfulness as an extended exorcism, banishing away all that is evil and uniting us with all that is good.

---

10 *Services of Initiation into the Holy Orthodox-Catholic and Apostolic Church* (LaVerne, CA: Antiochian Orthodox Institute, 2017), 37–38.

CHAPTER 8

Routing the Gods

And Jesus came and said to them, "All authority in heaven and on earth has been given to me. Go therefore and make disciples of all nations, baptizing them in the name of the Father and of the Son and of the Holy Spirit, teaching them to observe all that I have commanded you. And behold, I am with you always, to the end of the age."

—Matthew 28:18–20

This Son of Man whom you have seen is the One who would remove the kings and the mighty ones from their comfortable seats and the strong ones from their thrones. He shall loosen the reins of the strong and crush the teeth of the sinners. He shall depose the kings from their thrones and kingdoms.

—1 Enoch 46:4–5[1]

1 1 Enoch, 34.

We saw in chapter 5 how the nations had come to worship demonic fallen angels in the wake of the events at Babel, a relationship cemented through idolatry. Before the coming of Jesus Christ, Israel had to contend with the paganism of the ancient Near East—Canaanite, Akkadian, Sumerian, Mesopotamian, and so on. Thus, Jesus was born into the context of a world dominated by demonic oppression. His coming therefore heralded the doom of this ancient oppression:

> Thus all magic was dissolved and every bond of wickedness vanished; ignorance was abolished and the old kingdom was destroyed, since God was becoming manifest in human form for the newness of eternal life; what had been prepared by God had its beginning. Hence everything was shaken together, for the abolition of death was being planned.[2]

This "old kingdom" was precisely the kingdom of the demonic powers, characterized by ignorance, enslavement to wickedness, and magic. Christ's coming was about the abolition of death, the defeat of "the last enemy" (1 Cor. 15:26).

That is why, after Jesus rose from the dead, He sent out His apostles to participate in His reclamation of the world. The authority God had given to the angelic guardians who fell into evil after Babel was given back to Christ, which is why He links that return of authority with the word *therefore* when He sends the apostles out. That is, because He has taken the authority back from the demons, He can now re-delegate it to the apostles. They are the new patrons and guardians of the nations. A fundamental change in the order of the world happens with the coming of Christ. As His Mother prophesied, God has

2 Saint Ignatius of Antioch, *To the Ephesians*, trans. Robert M. Grant, in *The Apostolic Fathers*, ed. Jack N. Sparks (Nashville: Thomas Nelson, 1978), 83.

"brought down the mighty from their thrones / and exalted those of humble estate" (Luke 1:52), meaning that Christ has deposed the demons and has exalted humans to take up this position.

That said, however, even though the enemy has suffered the critical blow by Christ, demons are not yet absent from this world. The period in which we now live is a time between this decisive victory by Christ at His Resurrection and the end. Christ ascended into heaven and sat on His throne next to His Father, but He now "rule[s] in the midst of [His] enemies" (Ps. 110:2). He rules there until all His enemies are defeated and made a footstool for His feet (Ps. 110:1; Luke 20:43; Acts 2:35; Heb. 1:13, 10:13). Thus, when the apostles went out into the world, they continued to encounter paganism, the activity of demons among humankind. In our own time, even though ancient pagan religious traditions have been eliminated from most of the world, demons are still active among humans.

Along these lines, we might think of the rise of neopaganism. Neopaganism is the attempt to reconstruct ancient paganism, emphasizing its gods and often including a nature-focused theme. In most cases, neopaganism is actually quite distinct from ancient paganism in that it doesn't typically include animal sacrifice (though in some cases, it does). Even when there is animal sacrifice, however, rituals used for the purpose are new inventions, since the practice of these rituals ended many centuries ago without records detailing how they were performed. Further, Christian ethics is generally imported into neopaganism.

As one example of this ethical importation, neopagans generally treat women and children as full human persons who have the right of consent, equal to men. Ancient paganism did not treat them that way, and Greek pagan philosophy, for instance, regarded females essentially as defective males.[3] This viewpoint is part of why they

3 Aristotle, *On the Generation of Animals*, II.3.

were treated as property, often with horrifically brutal implications. Women and children as fully and equally human is a Christian concept, not a pagan one.[4] That neopagans would import Christian ethics into their reconstruction of paganism shows how radical the coming of Christ was.

The presence of demons among humans does not appear only in self-conscious neopaganism, however. Any sinful activity is a cooperation with demonic powers. Even though the demons have been cast down from their thrones, like any retreating army, they are hacking and burning as they go, pillaging what they can from the humans whom God is rescuing from their occupation. Because we have not yet reached the time when all of Christ's enemies have been put at His feet, like the apostles we still have to contend with demons and their evil. We see this contention in the New Testament, and we also see it in the history of Christianity that follows even to our own time. Thus, we will now examine how that contention has occurred both in the New Testament Scriptures and in the centuries following.

I will largely limit myself in this chapter to examples from Greek and Indo-European paganism. Why? Certainly, there are many other pagan traditions in the world we could discuss, but I am focusing on Indo-European traditions, particularly Germanic, for two main reasons. First, they are what I know best. Second and more importantly, however, these are the traditions that have most deeply influenced and informed the English language and the cultures that use it.

---

4 Aristotle, for instance, writes: "the male is by nature superior, and the female inferior; and the one rules, and the other is ruled; this principle, of necessity, extends to all mankind" (*Politics*, I.5) and "the freeman rules over the slave after another manner from that in which the male rules over the female, or the man over the child; although the parts of the soul are present in all of them, they are present in different degrees" (I.13).

Zeus and the New Testament

Because the events of the New Testament are largely situated within the Greek-speaking areas of the Roman Empire, the worship of the Greek gods is the most visible of the pagan traditions the New Testament mentions. A full examination of paganism in this time and place from the Scriptures and history would take a large study, so we will mainly limit ourselves here to looking at one example—Zeus.[5] Zeus is the most high god of the Greek pagan pantheon. Despite this prominence, the New Testament mentions him by name only in one place—Acts 14, where the people of Lystra identify St. Barnabas as Zeus and try to sacrifice to him.

In Greek paganism, Zeus is a thunder god, the son of an incestuous marriage between the Titan siblings Cronus and Rhea. Because he had received a prophecy that one of his children would overthrow him, Cronus cannibalistically consumes his children as they are born from Rhea, but she saves Zeus through tricking Cronus by giving him a stone in the baby's place. Fulfilling the prophecy, Zeus then becomes the most high god by launching the Titanomachy—killing his father, releasing his siblings from their father's belly, and then defeating the remaining Titans, locking them in Tartarus forever, the deepest part of the underworld.

After the Titanomachy, the great multi-headed serpentine monster Typhon, a child of Gaia and the god Tartarus, challenges Zeus's control over the cosmos.[6] With his thunderbolt, Zeus defeats the monster and sends him down into Tartarus as well. Zeus sets up his kingdom by dividing the world between himself and his brothers Poseidon and

5 For a detailed look at how the Roman Empire went from its centuries-long paganism to conversion to Christianity, see Robin Lane Fox's *Pagans and Christians* (New York: Alfred A. Knopf, Inc., 1989).

6 As we saw in ch. 4, to be dead is to be in the control of a death god, which is why *Tartarus* is the name of both a primordial deity and the abysmal depth over which he rules.

Hades, who receive rule over the seas and underworld, respectively. Zeus sets up his own throne on Mount Olympus to govern the heavens. He cements his hold on power when he successfully leads the Gigantomachy in response to an uprising against the Olympian gods by the giants, whom his grandmother Gaia had sent against him.[7]

He is famously a serial rapist and adulterer, begetting numerous demigod children with mortal women. He also had a series of marriages, most of them incestuous. His most famous divine wife is Hera, mother of Ares and Hephaestus, but she was his seventh wife and also his older sister. According to Hesiod, Zeus's first six wives were the nymph Metis (whom he swallows; they have a daughter, Athena, who emerges from his head), his aunt the Titan Themis (from whom are born the Seasons and Fates), another nymph named Eurynome (mother of the Graces), his sister Demeter (from whom is born Persephone[8]), his aunt the Titan Mnemosyne (mother of the Nine Muses), and finally another Titan named Leto (mother of Apollo and Artemis).

We can thus see that the character of Zeus is vile and immoral—even by pagan ethics (which were generally against incest, for instance). Why would Greek pagans worship such a being? Because they earnestly believed that he was the most high god, so the worship they offered to him was essentially of the sort of the obedience offered to an earthly king—in fear, and sometimes hope of receiving favors. We could examine the character of other pagan Greek gods—Hera is famously nasty and vindictive, Ares is of course violence personified, etc. But Zeus should suffice for our purpose, which is to give

---

7 The giants of Greek myth, offspring of Gaia, were born from the blood that fell to the ground when Zeus's father Cronus castrated his own father Ouranos during his violent rise to the status of most high god.

8 You may recall from the previous chapter that Hades abducts Persephone to marry her. She is of course his niece, both through his brother Zeus and his sister Demeter.

some context for Christ's appearance and the apostles's mission from Him. So why is this context important? It is important because the world into which the gospel was first preached is a world that actually worshiped violent, incestuous, rapist demons. Not only did it worship these beings, but these are the stories people actually told about them, the poetry they wrote about them, the images they painted and carved. Human artists directed their highest aspirations toward these demons.

The first Christians lived in a world where this worship was ever-present. Thus, Christ's letter to the Christians of Pergamon in Asia Minor, as related to the Apostle John, refers to Zeus, though without naming him: "'I know where you dwell, where Satan's throne is. Yet you hold fast my name, and you did not deny my faith even in the days of Antipas my faithful witness, who was killed among you, where Satan dwells'" (Rev. 2:13). What is "Satan's throne"? In Pergamon, there was a great temple to Zeus with a massive altar dedicated to the god. Constructed in the second century BC, it is roughly 117 feet (36 meters) wide and 110 feet (33 meters) deep, with its base decorated with a frieze depicting the Gigantomachy. It is U-shaped, with steps 65 feet (20 meters) wide leading up to the center between the two arms of the structure.[9] The altars of gods are commonly referred to as "thrones," so when Christ refers to "Satan's throne" when He speaks to the Pergamite Christians, He is identifying Zeus with Satan.

Apologetics on the Areopagus

With all this demonic evil surrounding Christians, and with an unmistakable association of the Greek pagans' most high god with the great demonic adversary of humankind, it is no wonder that St.

9 The structure was excavated in the late nineteenth century and is now on display at the Pergamon Museum in Berlin.

Paul spends so much time addressing paganism in his letters to Christians who have converted from paganism and still live in pagan contexts. He not only warns them against eating the sacrifices of idolatry (1 Cor. 10:20–21) and against the sexual immorality of paganism (1 Cor. 6:9–20), but he also warns them against falling back into the old ritual patterns of pagan life (Gal. 4:8–11). But is utter opposition the only way the New Testament addresses paganism?

Besides the abortive sacrifice in Acts 14 and the altar throne in Revelation 2, the New Testament mentions Zeus in another place without naming him, when St. Paul quotes two lines from Greek poets in Acts 17:28. The context in Acts 17 is St. Paul's address to the pagans on the Areopagus (Mars Hill) in Athens. Note the name of the place—it is named for the war god Ares. Why is it called this? Not because Ares was worshiped there but rather because in Athenian tradition, he was put on trial there by the other gods for killing the son of Hephaestus. So when the pagan philosophers and city governing council gathered there, they would have understood themselves as participating in the judgment function of the gods, joining themselves to that pagan divine council.

Why would St. Paul go to such a place? Acts 17:16 tells us: "Now while Paul was waiting for them at Athens, his spirit was provoked within him as he saw that the city was full of idols." He thus begins preaching Jesus Christ in the local synagogue and marketplace (17:17–18), speaking with both Jews and other devout people but also publicly with whomever would listen to him. Certain pagan philosophers notice this and bring him to make his presentation on their own "turf," the Areopagus (17:19–21). He accepts the invitation and goes to the Areopagus. Saint Paul's speech there is masterful as both a polemic against paganism and also as an apologetic for Christianity, following the pattern set in the Old Testament for both.

The apostle begins by complimenting the Athenians: "Men of Athens, I perceive that in every way you are very religious" (17:22).

Isn't this the man who six verses earlier was "provoked" in his spirit regarding Athenian idolatry? It is the same man, but he is crafting his message for his audience so that they can receive his words.

He continues: "For as I passed along and observed the objects of your worship, I found also an altar with this inscription: 'To the unknown god.' What therefore you worship as unknown, this I proclaim to you" (17:23). No doubt the pagan Athenians did not intend to worship Yahweh with that altar "to the unknown god" but were simply hedging their bets, spiritually speaking, hoping that if a god whom they did not know was angry at them, perhaps he might be placated by sacrifices offered there. Yet St. Paul has no problem using this pagan altar to a pagan god and repurposing it for his Christian apologetic. An altar intended for some unknown demon can become a figure to point people to the God of Israel.

Saint Paul goes on to preach how the God whom he serves created the whole world and is not limited by temples made by humans (17:24). God also does not need anything from humanity, because He is the source of all life and arranged everything so that humanity might seek Him out and find Him (17:25–27). He does not make it explicit here, but St. Paul is clearly contrasting God with the pagan gods, whom the pagans regard as dwelling in temples inside idols as bodies, as needing sacrifices, and as seeking after humanity to have their needs met. All these polemics against paganism are from the Old Testament, as we saw in chapter 1. As is written many times, who among the gods is like the Lord? None of them even claim to be like Him.

Immediately after setting up his critical frame for paganism, St. Paul quotes those lines from the Greek poets: "'In him we live and move and have our being'; / as even some of your own poets have said, / 'For we are indeed his offspring'" (17:28). The quotations are from two different sources but must have been well-known to the Athenians, and they also reveal the educational breadth of the apostle.

The first quotation ("in him . . .") is likely from Epimenides of Crete (sixth or seventh century BC), who in his *Cretica* has King Minos say to Zeus:

> They fashioned a tomb for you, holy and high one,
> Cretans, always liars, evil beasts, idle bellies.
> But you are not dead: you live and abide forever,
> For in you we live and move and have our being."[10]

The second is from Aratus (about 315–240 BC):

> From Zeus let us begin; him do we mortals never leave unnamed;
> full of Zeus are all the streets and all the market-places of men;
> full is the sea and the havens thereof;
> always we all have need of Zeus.
> For we are also his offspring.[11]

After using these two lines from pagan poetry about Zeus, St. Paul then says, "Being then God's offspring, we ought not to think that the divine being is like gold or silver or stone, an image formed by the art and imagination of man" (17:29). Thus, in this one sentence, he both appropriates language from pagan poetry and then also corrects

---

10 https://intertextual.bible/text/epimenides-cretica-1-acts-17.28. Saint Paul references the saying that all Cretans are liars in Titus 1:12. These lines from Epimenides survive in a ninth-century Syriac commentary on *Acts* by Isho'dad of Merv (a bishop of the Assyrian Church of the East), and St. John Chrysostom also quotes from them in his *Homily 3 on Titus*. The "lie" that Minos says Cretans tell about Zeus is that he is mortal.

11 Aratus of Soli, *Phaenomena*, in *Callimachus, Hymns and Epigrams*, trans. A. W. Mair and G R. Mair (London: William Heinemann, 1921), https://www.theoi.com/Text/AratusPhaenomena.html, 1–5.

the pagan approach by saying that God—unlike Zeus or other pagan gods—is not like any man-made image.

Saint Paul's final recorded words to the pagans on the Areopagus carry the call to action:

> The times of ignorance God overlooked, but now he commands all people everywhere to repent, because he has fixed a day on which he will judge the world in righteousness by a Man whom he has appointed; and of this he has given assurance to all by raising him from the dead. (Acts 17:30–31)

In one stroke, the apostle offers God's forgiveness to the pagans, who have lived in "the times of ignorance," but now that they know about the true God who created all things, the time has come to repent. He then leaves them with a suggestive reference to Christ, the "Man whom he has appointed" to judge the whole world, the proof being that He rose from the dead. Why is the Resurrection important here? If there is a God who raises the dead and who will righteously judge all the world, then He is clearly more powerful than any god whom the pagans worshiped, none of whom ever made such claims about themselves.

From St. Paul's words on the Areopagus, therefore, we see that he is doing what we saw in the previous chapter. As St. Justin would say, "there seem to be seeds of truth among all men." Also, as St. Basil would say, St. Paul is making use of pagan writings "after the manner of bees," carrying away what is good and leaving the rest.

Why does St. Paul do this? Why not simply blast the pagans with everything they get wrong, condemning them for their wickedness, for worshiping demons, for oppressing women, children, and slaves? Saint Paul is carrying out his own principle: "I have become all things to all people, that by all means I might save some" (1 Cor. 9:22). He speaks to them with their own imagery so that he can bring them to salvation in Christ, and because everything that is true belongs to God, there is no problem with using even pagan language to point to Christ. Even though Christianity is now beginning its ascendance over paganism, the apostle remains firmly in the tradition established in the Old Testament for how God's people ought to approach pagans.

Killing the Dragon[12]

What we see in the New Testament approach to pagan religion continues the Old Testament's approach, and we can see that the Church Fathers continue this same tradition. The mission is to rescue pagans from paganism, and when pagans say something good, that is used to bring them to Christ. When they say something bad, that is critiqued and corrected. By this means, the demons who oppress pagans through paganism are robbed of their prize—human worship. To demonstrate how this pattern continues, let's look at one of the great motifs of paganism, which I mentioned briefly when looking at the Zeus stories—divine dragon slaying. This motif continues in other forms of paganism as well, particularly in Germanic mythology and other legendary material.[13] We can find classic examples in Norse texts and in the poem *Beowulf.* With both these sources, the authors of the extant texts are Christians. *Beowulf* is a poem about pagans written by a Christian, but why would Christians write down and preserve stories originating with Norse paganism?

---

12 Portions of the following section are adapted from my unpublished 2022 academic paper titled "'The doom of the great gods': Dragons in Germanic myth and legend interpreted by J. R. R. Tolkien through the lens of eschatological Christian sources."

13 The dragon-killing motif is found throughout Indo-European paganism and other pagan traditions, but I am using Germanic examples here because they are likely most familiar to the English-speaking reader.

With a handful of exceptions, one could ask this question about nearly any form of pagan literature, which remains extant to our own day because of the work of Christians who invested great time and expense to hand copy pagan texts—usually in monasteries, no less! The purpose was not, of course, to promote worshiping pagan gods—notably, instructions for how to do so are nowhere preserved in this literature. Rather, the purpose was to go looking for St. Justin's "seeds of truth" everywhere, to use these texts to point toward Christ. In other words, they were continuing to do what the Old Testament prophets did, what the New Testament apostles did, and what the Church Fathers did. Christians kept these stories or composed them because they believed they could be used to serve Christ.

So, with this framework in mind, given the particular example of dragon slaying, let's look at what they did. We will use the examples of the dragon Fáfnir of the *Völsunga saga* and the Eddas, Beowulf's bane from the climax of his tale, and finally the Midgard serpent defeated by Thor.

Fáfnir appears in both the Eddas and also the prose *Völsunga saga* with essentially the same story.[14] When we look at all three sources, we see that the essentials of the story are these: Fáfnir and his brother Regin kill their father Hreidmar in order to get his cache of cursed gold.[15] The dwarf Andvari had obtained the gold as weregild for their brother Otter who had been killed by the gods Odin, Loki, and Hønir. After the brothers get hold of the gold, Fáfnir transforms himself into a dragon and guards the gold jealously without sharing it with Regin. Regin convinces the heroic Sigurd to slay Fáfnir so that they can split

14 Jackson Crawford, trans. and ed., *The Saga of the Volsungs with The Saga of Ragnar Lothbrok* (Indianapolis: Hackett Publishing Company, 2017), 25–35; Snorri Snurluston, *Edda*, trans. and ed. Anthony Faulkes (London: Everyman, 1987), 99–102; Carolyne Larrington, trans., *The Poetic Edda* (Oxford: Oxford University Press, 2014), 147–161.

15 Notably, in the *Völsunga saga*, Regin tells Sigurd that Fáfnir alone killed their father (Crawford, 26).

the gold. After Sigurd rams his sword into Fáfnir from below, he and Regin have a conversation while Fáfnir dies, concluding thus:

> Fáfnir said, "You will ride there, and find all the gold, and it will be enough for all your days. And that gold will kill you, and everyone else who owns it."
>
> Sigurð stood up and said, "I'd ride home and leave this treasure alone, if I knew that I would never die. But every bold man wants to have control of his wealth until his fated deathday.
>
> "And you, Fáfnir, lie there in your life's broken pieces, and may Hel have you." And with this, Fáfnir died.[16]

Sigurd exits the dragon's cave, and he and Regin proceed to cut up the dragon to eat it. Regin drinks the blood while Sigurd tastes some of the heart while it is cooking. This taste gives him the ability to understand the language of birds, and he hears birds talking with each other about how Regin is going to betray him. He thus turns and kills Regin, getting the cursed gold for himself.

A Christian reading of this tale, especially in light of Genesis 3–4, might immediately connect the serpent in Eden with Fáfnir but also with his brother Regin, a divine being who tempts the hero. Further, both point to a treasure—one guarding, the other tempted toward—that curses the one who takes it, as the serpent points Eve to the forbidden fruit. One brother murders another, as in Genesis 4 with Cain and Abel. Finally, the result of the confrontation is that the dragon is sent to the underworld.

The other great dragon of Norse myth, Jörmungandr, the Midgard serpent (*Miðgarðsormr*), has the god Thor as his primary opponent, as related in the Eddas. The two best-known encounters are when Thor brings the serpent up out of the sea during a fishing

16 Crawford, 33.

expedition, and of course the final confrontation at Ragnarok. These two sources mention both encounters only very briefly, but they become iconic nonetheless.

We find the fishing expedition in stanzas 21–24 of "Hymir's Poem" in the *Poetic Edda* (77). Thor baits his hook with an ox head and lowers it into the water, attracting "the one whom the gods hate, the All-Lands-Girdler." Thor pulls the head of the serpent up into the boat, strikes it with his hammer, then lets it sink back into the sea.[17] The whole narrative is reminiscent of the references in the Bible to taming Leviathan and even drawing him up with a hook (Job 41:1).

A brief mention of the final battle between Thor and the Midgard serpent at Ragnarok appears in the "Seeress's Prophecy" (*Voluspa*) in the *Poetic Edda*: "Then comes Hlodyn's glorious boy: / Odin's son advances to fight the serpent, / he strikes in wrath Midgard's-protector, / all men must abandon their homesteads; / nine steps Fiorgyn's child takes, / exhausted, from the serpent which fears no shame."[18] The prose *Edda* has a fuller treatment:

> [Odin] will make for Fenriswolf, and Thor will advance at his side and be unable to aid him because he will have his hands full fighting the Midgard serpent. . . . Thor will be victorious over the Midgard serpent and will step away from it nine paces. Then he will fall to the ground dead from the poison which the serpent will spit at him. The wolf will swallow Odin. That will be the cause of his death.[19]

In this eschatological moment of the downfall of the gods, while Odin faces the wolf (who is the serpent's brother) and the wolf eats him, Thor kills the serpent yet ultimately dies because of poison. These themes of a final divine face-off with the monstrous serpent are

17 Larrington, *Poetic Edda*, 77; Snurluston, "Gylfaginning," *Edda*, 57.
18 Larrington, 11.
19 Snurluston, 54.

similar to those in Christian sources, but Thor dies while killing his foe and has no hope of return. Christ's defeat of the eschatological dragon, however, does include His own death but sees Him coming back to life and destroying the death-demon forever.

The final dragon we will mention here is the unnamed serpent, often called "Beowulf's bane," whose destruction by the hero is roughly the last third of the Old English poem *Beowulf* (lines 2200–3182). This dragon has many of the features we see with both biblical and Norse mythological dragons. It lives underground in a barrow, which associates it with the underworld. It guards a cursed treasure. It breathes fire like Leviathan and is a threat to the whole kingdom. Beowulf confronts the dragon alone and kills it, but like Thor, he ultimately dies in the process. Yet, while there is no resurrection for Beowulf in the poem, the end suggests some kind of spiritual future for him in that it details his funeral and how he will be remembered.[20]

In these tales, we see a continuity with dragons found in explicitly Christian sources after the New Testament. I discussed St. Basil's text on pagan literature in the last chapter, and he actually mentions dragons in a passing reference: "For of what use, now, are riches, if one scorns the pleasures of the flesh? I certainly see none, unless, as in the case of the mythological dragons, there is some satisfaction in guarding hidden treasure."[21] Here we see that St. Basil is not only aware of the tradition of dragons "guarding hidden treasure," but he associates dragons with the bald pleasure of desiring and possessing treasure. This image connects back to Genesis 3, in which the serpent is not so much guarding a treasure as tempting toward it, offering the object of desire as an end in itself rather than referring it to a higher purpose.

---

20 R. M. Liuzza, trans. and ed., *Beowulf* (Ontario: Broadview Editions, 2013), 115–144.

21 Saint Basil, "Address," IX.

In another Christian source, the seventh-century *Gospel of Pseudo-Matthew* (an extra-canonical and highly fanciful infancy gospel of Jesus), we read a tale of the young Jesus fleeing to Egypt with his Mother Mary, foster-father Joseph, and Joseph's children, a reference to the canonical Matthew 2:13–15.[22] In chapter 18, the family stops to rest in a cave, and dragons issue forth from it, frightening the other children. The two-year-old Jesus climbs down from his Mother and confronts the dragons. They bow before him and become tame, and the text says that this is a fulfillment of Psalm 148:7: "Praise the LORD from the earth, / you dragons; ye dragons, and all you deeps."[23]

Finally, the fourth- and fifth-century bishop and homilist St. John Chrysostom, in his *Homily XXIV on First Corinthians*,[24] describes what happened when Christ entered into Hades through his death on the Cross:

> And that which happened to the Babylonian dragon,[25] when, having taken the food it burst asunder in the midst, this also happened unto him. For Christ came not forth again by the mouth of death, but having burst asunder and ripped up in the very midst, the belly of the dragon, thus from His secret chambers right gloriously He issued

22 *Gospel of Pseudo-Matthew*, trans. Alexander Walker, in *Ante-Nicene Fathers*, eds. Alexander Roberts, James Donaldson, and A. Cleveland Coxe, vol. 8 (Peabody, MA: Hendrickson Publishers, 1999), 368–383.

23 *Pseudo-Matthew*, 376. The text quotes from the Greek Psalter, which uses *drakontes* ("dragons"); translations of the original Hebrew *tannin* variously read "sea creatures," "serpents," "sea monsters," and also "dragons."

24 Saint John Chrysostom, "Homily XXIV on First Corinthians," trans. Talbot W. Chambers, in *Nicene and Post-Nicene Fathers I*, ed. Philip Schaff, vol. 12 (Peabody, MA: Hendrickson Publishers, 1999), 138–143.

25 The "Babylonian dragon" to which Chrysostom alludes is featured in Bel and the Dragon, which I mentioned in ch. 7. This dragon, which was worshiped by local pagans, is fed cakes of pitch, fat, and hair by the prophet Daniel. Upon eating them, the dragon explodes (Bel and the Dragon, 23–27).

> forth and flung abroad His beams not to this heaven alone, but to the very throne most high. For even there did He carry it up.[26]

In Chrysostom's depiction, Christ enters into the mouth of the devouring dragon of death, and as it is feeling nauseated and wants to vomit, Christ rips it into pieces from the inside, not only escaping death but destroying its power forever. He uses similar imagery in his famed Paschal homily. Jesus here not only defeats the dragon but also brings out the treasure hidden within—He raises up the dead saints: "For when [Christ's body] was crucified, then were the dead raised up, then was that prison burst, and the gates of brass were broken, and the dead were loosed, and the keepers of hell-gate all cowered in fear."[27]

Christ looting the treasures held in Hades by the dragon is a theme found throughout Christian tradition—and perhaps most memorably in the Gospel of Nicodemus, which focuses especially on the Harrowing of Hades. Christian tradition also associates dragon slaying with both the Archangel Michael (due to the reference in Rev. 12:7) and St. George, whose hagiography famously includes dracomachy. Sometimes he kills the dragon and sometimes he tames it.

Integration of the Pagan into Christianity

To wrap up this chapter, I want to look briefly at a few examples of Christian culture that fully integrate pagan imagery into Christian objects. Here we see not only allusions to pagan literature, or the use of pagan titles and terminology, but clearly pagan images referring to pagan stories yet turned to the use of Christians to point to Jesus Christ.

I told the story above of the slaying of Fáfnir by Sigurd. This story appears on carved wooden doorposts that adorned the outside of

---

26 Chrysostom, "Homily XXIV," 142.

27 Chrysostom, 142.

the Hylestad Stave Church, a twelfth- or thirteenth-century church in Norway. The church itself no longer exists, but after it was demolished in the seventeenth century, the carvings were reused in other buildings and are now on display at the Museum of Cultural History in Oslo. Why would Norwegian Christians put these images on their church? I once had someone suggest to me that it was to lure in pagans, who would see Sigurd on the outside of the building then presumably enter and stay, even though the inside of the building was clearly Christian. This makes no sense, however, as the church was built centuries after the last Norse pagan was baptized into Christianity. There would have been no pagans around to be lured in by this facile religious bait and switch.

While you think about that question, consider another object—the Franks Casket.[28] This is a small box on display at the British Museum in London, likely made in the early eighth century in Northumbria (northern England). All indications are that it was monastic in origin. Its size and shape suggest that it might have been used as a reliquary. What is on this box? Some of the carved illustrations are hard to decipher, but the parts that have been successfully identified include a depiction of Romulus and Remus (founders of pagan Rome), the capture of Jerusalem by Titus (Roman general and later, emperor), Wayland the Smith (a semi-divine Germanic legendary figure also known as Volund or Weland), and the Adoration of Christ by the Magi. Here we have generally pagan images and one clearly Christian one. Again, what is going on here?

The Christians who made these objects included pagan imagery on them not to glorify the pagan gods or to encourage their worship.

---

28 The name refers to Sir Augustus Wollaston Franks, who bought parts of the casket in Paris in 1857 and donated it to the British Museum. It is also called the Auzon Casket, as another panel was found in the French village of Auzon (where all the pieces had been), which is on display at the Bargello Museum in Florence.

Indeed, as I have looked into this pre-modern phenomenon, I have not yet found images of actual gods. The closest one gets is ambiguous figures like Wayland. It seems to me that the Adoration of the Magi summarizes the purpose beautifully, in a story from Matthew 2:1–12. In this story, men from the east who are variously described as magicians, astrologers, wise men, or kings—who are certainly pagans—come to worship Jesus Christ, led by a miraculous star they saw and followed. It is an image of pagans who follow what they know and then encounter Christ, repenting and giving Him their worship.

For this same reason the author of *Beowulf* can refer to God as *alf walda* ("elf ruler") in line 1314 of this Old English poem. As a Christian who knew the Germanic pagan tradition well, he inherited the concept of "elves" from his cultural past. In this tradition, an elf is a spirit, an immaterial being who is part of the unseen population of the Germanic world. For the poet, therefore, the *walda* ("lord," "ruler") who is above them all is properly the *alf walda*—or, to put it another way, He is the Lord of spirits.

CHAPTER 9

The Sons of God

For I consider that the sufferings of this present time are not worth comparing with the glory that is to be revealed to us. For the creation waits with eager longing for the revealing of the sons of God.

—Romans 8:18–19

According to nature, then—that is, according to creation, so to speak—we are all sons of God, because we have all been created by God. But with respect to obedience and doctrine we are not all the sons of God: those only are so who believe in Him and do His will. And those who do not believe, and do not obey His will, are sons and angels of the devil, because they do the works of the devil.

—St. Irenaeus of Lyons[1]

1 Saint Irenaeus of Lyons, *Against Heresies* IV.41.2, in *Ante-Nicene Fathers*, trans. and eds. Alexander Roberts, James Donaldson, and A. Cleveland Coxe, vol. 1 (Peabody, MA: Hendrickson Publishers, 1999), 524–5.

CHRISTIANS ARE CALLED TO BE saints. It is the very purpose of Christian life. What does that mean, though? To understand the possibility of sanctity, it might help to consider its opposite. What is the opposite of a saint? It's not a question we consider very often. Typically, we juxtapose "sinners" with "saints." Since we know we're all sinners, which therefore seems ordinary, saints are people who are better than the rest of us. So we divide the spiritual world of humans into the ordinary and the special. But what is the opposite of an angel? This seems easier—the opposite of angels are demons.[2] They are fallen angels, and the holiness and glory of angels is juxtaposed with the evil and darkness of the demons. Here we do not see a division between ordinary and special but rather between glorious and diabolical.

So what if I told you it's possible for humans also to be dark and diabolical, to become like demons in their evil rebellion against God? It is a frightening thought, but it accords with our experience—at least with our experience as a human race in history. Some people have become so evil, so cruel, so self-indulgent that the scale of their sin has slaughtered millions. Why focus on this? My purpose here is not to spend time contemplating evil so that we might be fascinated at how deep into a human heart it truly can go. Rather, it is so that we might understand better what it really means to be a saint.

So what is actually the opposite of a saint? In the Bible, it's a giant.

The Nephilim

If there is a biblical story that above all others stirs up excitement, spawns conspiracy theories, inspires spiritual thrillers, and can

---

2 Strictly speaking, goodness does not have an "opposite." Evil is not a "thing" but is the distortion or privation of good, just as darkness is the privation of light. But I am not using this metaphysical frame but rather a phenomenological, experiential one.

dominate late-night alternative radio shows, it is the story in Genesis 6 about the rise of the giants. People get excited when you talk about giants—especially when you take them seriously. I believe in giants, because I believe in the reality of evil.

Here is how the biblical text describes the rise of the giants:

> When man began to multiply on the face of the land and daughters were born to them, the sons of God saw that the daughters of man were attractive. And they took as their wives any they chose. Then the LORD said, "My Spirit shall not abide in man forever, for he is flesh: his days shall be 120 years." The Nephilim were on the earth in those days, and also afterward, when the sons of God came in to the daughters of man and they bore children to them. These were the mighty men who were of old, the men of renown.
>
> The LORD saw that the wickedness of man was great in the earth, and that every intention of the thoughts of his heart was only evil continually. And the LORD regretted that he had made man on the earth, and it grieved him to his heart. So the LORD said, "I will blot out man whom I have created from the face of the land, man and animals and creeping things and birds of the heavens, for I am sorry that I have made them." (Gen. 6:1–7)

Whatever the Nephilim are, it is clear that the Bible's view of them is very dark indeed. God sees the rise of the giants as great wickedness, evidence of perpetually evil thoughts in humankind, and for this He will wipe them from the earth. What happens next is the story of the great Flood, when God spares only Noah and his family—eight people saved while the Flood destroys the rest of humanity.

How should we understand what is happening here? What are the giants? Why is their rise so evil that God destroys almost the entire human race?

What Is a Giant?

The word *Nephilim* (a loanword into Hebrew from Aramaic) literally means "giants." The Septuagint translation of the word affirms this translation as the right one, which is the Greek *gigantes,* from which our English word *giants* comes. The Scripture also identifies these giants with the Hebrew *gibborim* ("mighty ones") of old (Gen. 6:4), and the parallel in the Greek simply repeats *gigantes* here. In both cases, they are called "men of renown." These are powerful, famous men. Genesis, here, doesn't say anything about their size, though we do get references to size for later giants, such as Goliath, who is "six cubits and a span" (over nine feet tall) in the Hebrew text of the Scriptures (1 Sam. 17:4), but "four cubits and a span" (less than seven feet tall) in the Greek translation and in the Hebrew of the Dead Sea Scrolls. Numbers 13:33 does not mention their specific size, but the Hebrew spies say they feel like grasshoppers when they see them.

Were they supernaturally tall? Certainly, other texts in the tradition of Israel describe them as very large. 1 Enoch 7:2, for instance, says they are 300 cubits tall—about 450 feet. In the Testaments of the Twelve Patriarchs 3:7, one of the giants is twelve cubits high (about eighteen feet). The variation in height among sources suggests that the point is not that they were a physically tall, enhanced species of demi-human, but rather that size here is symbolic of something else. Indeed, other ancient Greek texts use *gigas* ("giant") to refer to powerful, tyrannical human rulers—so it is roughly like our English use of *strongman* or even *giant,* which can be metaphorical, not necessarily referring to someone of great size and strength. So why use size as a symbol? It is not only to refer to their power and influence but also, as we will see, to associate them with divine beings, whom ancient cultures almost uniformly depicted as extremely tall.

We need to note that giants show up after the Flood and not only before: "The Nephilim were on the earth in those days, *and also afterward*." The Bible references Nephilim in other places in the Old Testament as well, such as Numbers 13:33, which uses the same word to refer to the Anakim who inhabited the land of Canaan, whom Israel encountered after the Exodus. The Old Testament also identifies other groups of people in this same category with similar language, such as the Rephaim, Amorites, Zamzummim, Emim, and Amalekites. The *gibborim* language also reappears in a variety of places, for example, when it refers to the hunter Nimrod in Genesis 10:9, who in the Greek is called a *gigas*. So whatever Nephilim are, they are destroyed and yet reappear later. Let's talk briefly about their origins.[3]

The Origin of Giants

We should now ask who the "sons of God" are. We have already seen that in the Scriptures the phrase *sons of God* usually refers to angels,[4] so with that reading, the giants are in some way the offspring of spiritual beings and humans. Ancient pagan religions of course have a category for this, usually rendered in English as *demigod*.[5] A number

3 For another treatment of this question, especially including the place of gigantomachy in the Scriptures, see Fr. Stephen De Young's *The Religion of the Apostles*, 90–96, and *God is a Man of War*, 69–78 (both from Ancient Faith Publishing, 2021).

4 Julius Africanus, in his *Chronographiai* 2, mentions that he has seen Greek texts of Gen. 6:4 that use *sons of God*, after himself referring to "angels of God," suggesting that some use the latter rather than the former. Saint Augustine, in *City of God* XV.23, mentions that the Aquila Greek translation reads "sons of the gods." Saint Cyril of Alexandria notes this Aquila reading and also that the Symmachus uses "sons of the rulers" (*Glaphyra in Genesis* 2.1).

5 The Latin equivalent *semideus* and Greek *hemitheos* in ancient sources are not consistent with our modern *demigod* concept, part-human and part-divine. These words sometimes get used for fully divine beings who are merely lesser

of figures in mythological tales have both divine and mortal parents, such as the Greek Heracles (son of Zeus and the mortal Alcmene), Theseus (son of Poseidon and the mortal Aethra), and the Irish Cú Chulainn (son of the god Lugh and the mortal Deichtine). Usually we think of them as half-god and half-human, and they are typically also called *heroes*. Within their stories, they demonstrate their greatness by the magnificence of their heroic feats.

This approach to understanding the origin of giants in Genesis 6—that the "sons of God" are rebellious angels—occurs in several places in Second Temple Jewish literature. Typical is this passage from the Book of Jubilees:[6]

> And when the children of men began to multiply on the surface of the earth and daughters were born to them, that the angels of the LORD saw in a certain year of that jubilee that they were good to look at. And they took wives for themselves from all of those whom they chose. And they bore children for them; and they were the giants. (Jub. 5:1)[7]

Though it is not explicit in the New Testament, texts such as these from St. Jude can be read in this way:

> And the angels who did not stay within their own position of authority, but left their proper dwelling, he has kept in eternal chains under

spirits. As we saw in chapter 1, the concept of *god* in most ancient contexts was not so much a species as a way of referring to a divine ruler. The English *demigod* itself has not always been consistent, e.g., John Milton in *Paradise Lost* uses *demigod* to refer to angels.

6 Other examples from this literature include 1 Enoch 6:2, 7:2; Jubilees 7:21–22; Book of Giants G; Testament of the Twelve Patriarchs I.5; and the Damascus Document 2:17–18. All of these texts were found among the Dead Sea Scrolls. It is also found in Philo of Alexandria's *On the Giants* and *Questions* (ca. 20 BC–AD 50); 2 Baruch 56:10–14, a Jewish text (AD 70–100); and Josephus's *Antiquities of the Jews*, ch. 3.

7 Jubilees, 64.

> gloomy darkness until the judgment of the great day—just as Sodom and Gomorrah and the surrounding cities, which likewise indulged in sexual immorality and pursued unnatural desire, serve as an example by undergoing a punishment of eternal fire.
>
> It was also about these that Enoch, the seventh from Adam, prophesied, saying, "Behold, the Lord comes with ten thousands of his holy ones, to execute judgment on all and to convict all the ungodly of all their deeds of ungodliness that they have committed in such an ungodly way, and of all the harsh things that ungodly sinners have spoken against him." (Jude 6–7, 14–15)

Here, Jude refers to fallen angels chained deep in the underworld for their ancient sin, and likens it directly to the sexual immorality of Sodom and Gomorrah.[8] Note also how Jude quotes directly from Enoch, in which this same story is found in detail. Saint Peter mentions these same events, connecting them with the Flood, as does almost every ancient Jewish and Christian text:

> For if God did not spare angels when they sinned, but cast them into hell [Greek *Tartaros*] and committed them to chains of gloomy darkness to be kept until the judgment; if he did not spare the ancient world, but preserved Noah, a herald of righteousness, with seven others, when he brought a flood upon the world of the ungodly. (2 Pet. 2:4–5)

Saint Peter's use of *Tartaros* also connects the biblical account with the Greek pagan story of the Titans, who are also chained in this deepest part of the underworld.

---

8 With this interpretation, the sin of Sodom and Gomorrah in Genesis 19 goes beyond sexual immorality between humans to what is, within the text, literally an attempt to engage in sexual relations with the two angels God sent to take Lot out of Sodom.

A number of early Christian texts interpret the Genesis text this same way, such as this one from St. Irenaeus of Lyons:[9] [10]

> And for a very long while wickedness extended and spread, and reached and laid hold upon the whole race of mankind, until a very small seed of righteousness remained among them: and illicit unions took place upon the earth, since angels were united with the daughters of the race of mankind; and they bore to them sons who for their exceeding greatness were called giants. And the angels brought as presents to their wives teachings of wickedness, in that they brought them the virtues of roots and herbs, dyeing in colors and cosmetics, the discovery of rare substances, love-potions, aversions, amours, concupiscence, constraints of love, spells of bewitchment, and all sorcery and idolatry hateful to God; by the entry of which things into the world evil extended and spread, while righteousness was diminished and enfeebled.[11]

There are also patristic texts, mostly from later centuries, that disagree with this interpretation and instead say that the "sons of God"

---

9 Other examples from early Christian literature include St. Ambrose of Milan, *Treatise on Noah and David* IV.8; St. Athenagoras, *A Plea for the Christians* 24; Clementine Homily VIII, 15; Commodianus, *On Christian Discipline* 3; Eusebius of Caesarea, *Preparation for the Gospel* 5.4; Julius Africanus, *Chronographiai* Fragment 2 (also includes Sethite reading); St. Justin Martyr, *Second Apology* 5; Lactantius, *Divine Institutes* 2.15; Sulpitius Severus, *Sacred History* I.2; and Tertullian, *On the Apparel of Women* I.2.

10 The third-century Christian writer Origen (condemned as a heretic in the sixth century) mentions without endorsement an interpretation that the "sons of God" are preexisting human souls who descended into women and produced the giants (*Commentary on the Gospel of John*, 25). He mentions this interpretation again in *Contra Celsum* 5.54, using it to refute Celsus but still without endorsing it. Despite this lack of endorsement, the interpretation generally fits into his heretical system of the preexistence of souls.

11 Saint Irenaeus of Lyons, *Proof, 18*.

of Genesis 6 are the descendants of Seth (the "Sethite" reading). An example is this one from St. John Cassian:[12]

> From the sons of Seth and daughters of Cain, then, as we have said, still more wicked sons were begotten who were powerful hunters, very violent and savage men. On account of their huge bodies and their great cruelty and maliciousness they were called giants. (VIII.21)[13]

On the one hand, therefore, we have Jewish and Christian interpretations of the giants' fathers as fallen angelic beings, which is essentially the same narrative as in pagan mythology—unions between humans and divine beings producing some kind of heroic, hybrid offspring. The pagan tales see this as positive, but the biblical account views it as profoundly negative.

The other interpretation, generally from later Christian texts, is that the giants' fathers are fully human descendants of Seth and Cain. These texts do not really explain how such a union produces giants, however.[14] One way of dealing with the contradiction between these two interpretations is to say that the Church's view on the matter evolved or settled on the Sethite reading later in history: that early texts and Fathers were simply wrong about this but later ones got it right.

---

12 Other examples from later Christian literature include St. Augustine of Hippo, *City of God* 15.23; St. Ephraim the Syrian, *Commentary on Genesis,* VI.3–5; St. John Chrysostom, *Homilies on Genesis* 22; Julius Africanus, *Chronographiai* Fragment 2 (also includes angelic reading); and Theodoret of Cyrus, *On Genesis, Questions on the Octateuch* XLVII.

13 Saint John Cassian, *The Conferences,* trans. Boniface Ramsey (New York: Paulist Press, 1997), 307.

14 Saint Ephraim says that Seth's descendants were physically larger than Cain's, because they were closer to God and to Paradise (*Commentary on Genesis,* VI.5–6). One might think this means that Seth's line are the giants and that union with Cainites would result in half-giants. He does not elaborate, unfortunately.

Yet is it possible to reconcile these two views? Is there some way of reading all these texts such that both the earlier and later writers all point to the same reality, or that at least their reasoning in itself is not contradictory? Saint John Cassian provides a gateway into this possibility:

> Since by God's design a reading from Genesis was produced a little while ago which made such a significant impression on us that now we can pursue properly what we have always wanted to learn, we also wish to know what should be thought about those apostate angels that are said to have had intercourse with the daughters of men. Understood literally, would this be possible for a spiritual nature? . . .
>
> By no means should it be believed that spiritual natures can have carnal relations with women. But if this could ever have happened in a literal sense, why does it not occur now, at least occasionally, and why do we not see some people born of women without sexual intercourse, having been conceived by demons? (VIII.20–21)[15]

Cassian's reasoning here, that it is impossible for spiritual beings to have children with material beings like women, gets repeated in most of the texts that adopt the Sethite view and reject the angelic reading. That angels cannot reproduce is consistent with what we saw in chapter 2 from St. John of Damascus. This reasoning therefore precludes a strictly literal reading of both the Genesis 6 account of the origin of giants and also the pagan accounts of half-human, half-divine demigod heroes.

Is it possible to maintain this idea that angels cannot mate with humans while also affirming the earlier reading? Saint John's question gives us the possibility: "why does it not occur now, at least

---

15 Saint John Cassian, *Conferences*, 304.

occasionally, and why do we not see some people born of women without sexual intercourse, having been conceived by demons?" It seems that St. John also argues against this idea by saying, effectively, "This couldn't have happened, because we don't see it happening now."

How does this help? To understand that, first we have to remember that by the time St. John was writing in southeastern Gaul (modern France) in the late fourth and early fifth century, paganism was dying, and absent from most places near him or from places he would have heard about. That means he would not have had much testimony of pagan practices. To use our language from chapter 7, pagan myth had become mythology—they were stories told that no one participated in ritually.

Further, we do have evidence from within ancient Near Eastern paganism and also from the Bible of ritual practices that can fit both the sense that the giants are fully human and also that demons are somehow involved in their conception. Pagan demigods and biblical giants can indeed be the same thing, and Christians continued to accept that association for centuries even after the death of paganism. For instance, Alfred the Great's ninth-century translation of Boethius's *Consolation of Philosophy* makes explicit the association of biblical giants with pagan demigods when, in the section where Boethius briefly alludes to giants, Alfred expands it considerably by saying that the biblical account is a correction of the pagan one about the Titans.[16]

If it's not possible for the divine and human to reproduce, how can fallen angels mate with humans? A clue to the solution to this conundrum lies, oddly enough, with Og, whom the biblical text

---

16 *Alfred the Great's Boethius*, accessed November 4, 2021, http://www.uky.edu/~kiernan/ENG720/SdgTrans/SedgefieldProseTrans.htm. Alfred also says that the giant Nimrod built the Tower of Babel, connecting giants with the evils that followed.

does not say is a survivor of the Flood. What it does say about him, however, is that he has an enormous bed—over thirteen feet long—in the same verse that describes him as one of the Rephaim, a giant-clan (Deut. 3:11).

Why would Og have an enormous bed? On the one hand, one might assume that it had to be so large because he was a giant. Upon closer examination, however, it becomes apparent that the size of the bed is based in ancient pagan ritual.[17] Gods were almost uniformly depicted in ancient traditions as being around twelve to fifteen feet tall. In some rituals, the kings of these giant-clans—who were themselves understood to be divine beings—would embody the god their tribe worshiped. Then they would climb into the bed with a temple prostitute and engage in sexual relations. Thus the bed was large not to accommodate superhumanly tall kings but rather—in a ritual way—to accommodate gods. This ritual is known as *hierogamy* (from the Greek *hieros gamos*, "sacred marriage").

Children born from these unions were understood to have two divine parents (the god-king and the god) and one human one (the prostitute). So, from a ritual point of view, these children were two thirds divine and one third human, while from a biological point of view, they were fully human, since they had two human parents (the king and the prostitute). Thus, they were both ordinary humans, genetically speaking, but in some way charged with demonic power because of dark spiritual practices, a power that continued and developed through a life of demon worship that followed.

A ritual bed of this type has been unearthed in a place called Etemenanki, where worship of the Babylonian Marduk took place at a ziggurat there.[18] There are also references to such beds in pagan

17 Maria Lindquist, "King Og's Iron Bed," *The Catholic Biblical Quarterly* 73, no. 3 (July 2011): 477–492.

18 Lindquist, 480, footnote 12.

temples in a number of texts, such as in *Gilgamesh, Enkidu and the Netherworld,* a Sumerian text that long predates the *Epic of Gilgamesh* and mentions how the goddess Inanna sought to build a temple for herself that would contain both a throne (i.e., an altar) and a bed.[19]

Mesopotamian and Jewish traditions also track spirits they refer to variously as the "Seven Sages" or *apkallu,* which they understood to be antediluvian Watchers and their giant "sons" who did not bodily survive the Flood. These traditions say the apkallu transmitted antediluvian wisdom to various kings, who themselves claimed to be divine. Included among these esoteric secrets is weapons technology but also spells for seduction or for warding off evil spirits, and even for technology modern people might consider more mundane, such as for architecture or agriculture.[20] This account is basically what we see in the Enochian literature and from St. Irenaeus. Additionally, the Sumerian King List (known from clay cuneiform tablets and cylinders found in Mesopotamia) and also the Book of Giants (a text found among the Dead Sea Scrolls) list famous kings such as Gilgamesh as giants but also as closely associated with an apkallu, who gave them wisdom. Further, the texts refer to these kings as being two-thirds divine—an indication of their origins in the Nephilim ritual described above.

From a pagan point of view, therefore, these bed-related rituals produced heroes and god-kings who were empowered by their gods with divine favor and glory. From the biblical point of view, which refers to the gods of the nations as "demons," these were human

---

19 J. A. Black, G. Cunningham, E. Fluckiger-Hawker, E. Robson, and G. Zólyomi, *The Electronic Text Corpus of Sumerian Literature,* University of Oxford, http://etcsl.orinst.ox.ac.uk.

20 Amar Annus, "On the Origin of Watchers: A Comparative Study of the Antediluvian Wisdom in Mesopotamian and Jewish Traditions," *Journal for the Study of the Pseudepigrapha* 19, no. 4 (May 2010): 277–320.

beings who had become so demonized that they functioned like fallen angels. That giants came from pagan ritual rather than literal angelic genealogical descent explains why there can be giants both before and after the Flood and also how they can result from biologically human intercourse.

Demonized Humans

Ultimately, for my point here, it does not matter how one explains the origin of giants or even whether they were physically large or exhibited demonic powers. Nor does it matter which ancient or later text one endorses on this question. The point is that the events of Genesis 6 and the many other appearances of giants in the Old Testament all indicate one thing—it is possible for humans to descend very deeply into evil.

That might come as no particular surprise to those who know even just twentieth-century history, with its totalitarian slaughter of millions. We know that people can be evil. What may not be as apparent, however, is that this darkness is traditionally associated with demonic activity, and that the Orthodox Tradition has understood humans to have the possibility for demonization—not to turn into demons but to become functionally like them, even after death. What does this look like? Jubilees gives us a sense:

> And it came to pass when the children of men began to multiply on the face of the earth and daughters were born unto them, that the angels of God saw them on a certain year of this jubilee, that they were beautiful to look upon; and they took themselves wives of all whom they chose, and they bare unto them sons and they were giants.
>
> And injustice increased upon the earth, and all flesh corrupted its way; man and cattle and beasts and birds and everything which walks

> on the earth. And they all corrupted their way and their ordinances, and they began to eat one another. And injustice grew upon the earth and every imagination of the thoughts of all mankind was thus continually evil.
>
> And the LORD saw the earth, and behold it was corrupted and all flesh had corrupted its order and all who were on the earth had done every sort of evil in his sight. (Jub. 5:1–3)[21]

The corruption originally comes through the dark sexual immorality of unions with demons, but it can ultimately cause people to become more and more evil, resulting even in cannibalism. In this passage, the whole world grew to be full of every kind of evil; every human thought was evil, and it was so pervasive that it affected even the animals. God looked upon this evil and said that He would wipe humanity off the earth. This is an image of a humanity that has fallen into demonization.

No less a figure than St. John Chrysostom addresses this possibility of demonization. In one of his sermons, he refutes what seems to have been an urban legend of his time:

> For it is a fact that many of the less instructed think that the souls of those who die a violent death become wandering spirits [demons].
>
> But this is not so. I repeat it is not so. For not the souls of those who die a violent death become demons, but rather the souls of those who live in sin; not that their nature is changed, but that in their desires they imitate the evil nature of demons. Showing this very thing to the Jews, Christ said, "Ye are the children of the devil" [John 7:44]. He said that they were the children of the devil, not

21 Jubilees, 64.

> because they were changed into a nature like his, but because they performed actions like his. Wherefore also He adds: "For the lusts of your father ye will do."[22]

Here, "the less instructed" were saying that people could become demons if they die through violent means. Chrysostom does not say, "No, people can't become demons after death" but rather, effectively, "That's not how you become a demon after death." One becomes a demon after death by living like one before death—not changed in nature but certainly changed in mode of existence.

In one of his homilies, while Chrysostom says that demons dwelling around tombs are not the souls of dead humans,[23] clearly he also believes that humans can become truly demonic. Saint Gregory of Nyssa does, however, relate a speculation from his sister St. Macrina that apparitions one sees around tombs may well be in some way related to human souls who have not fully detached themselves from earthly things.[24] A number of early texts do, in any event, identify the "unclean spirits" the Scriptures mention as the human souls of dead giants, wandering the earth and tormenting human beings. This view not only appears in Jubilees 10:1–13 but also in the texts of a number of early Christian writers.[25] Why do the Scriptures call these spirits "unclean"? In the Torah, one of the categories of uncleanness was inappropriate hybridity, mixing together what should not be mixed. If giants are the result in some way of

22 Saint John Chrysostom, *Four discourses, chiefly on the parable of the Rich man and Lazarus* (London: Longmans, Green, Reader, and Dyer, 1869), discourse II, sec. 1, https://www.tertullian.org/fathers/chrysostom_four_discourses_02_discourse2.htm.

23 "Homily XXVIII on Matthew" (Matt. 28:3–4).

24 *On the Soul and the Resurrection.*

25 Saint Athenagoras, *A Plea for the Christians* 25; Clementine Homily VIII, 15–20; and Lactantius, *Divine Institutes* 2.15. The Clementine Homily also suggests in ch. 13 that fallen angels can in some sense become human.

unions between humans and fallen angels, then they fit this category of unclean hybridity.

What are we to make of this? Again, what one may believe about the nature or origin of unclean spirits or giants is not the point here, though as we have seen, there were various beliefs about this in the ancient world. My purpose is not to suggest that Christians are dogmatically required to believe any of these understandings. Rather, the point is that demonized humans—giants, however conceived[26]—are the opposite of saints. If saints are infused with the holiness, light, glory, love, and power of God because of their cooperation with Him in synergistic faithfulness, then it is also possible through cooperation with demons to become as though the devil were our father, doing his works and being filled with his malice, appetites, and violence (see John 8:39, 44). It is, in a word, anti-theosis, or to coin a term for this context, *demonosis.*

You Will Be Like Gods

Why bring all this up? Why introduce this final chapter with such darkness? For one thing, so that we might see what kind of evil Christ rescues His creation from. This book is about the framework for the spiritual war, and we cannot understand that war and fight it without having a sense of the risks to humans if the enemy defeats them.

More so, however, when we see this phrase *sons of God* in the Scriptures, we should have a sense of the spiritual power with which it is charged. The giants' way is the way of anti-theosis, a mockery and shortcut for becoming sons of God not through humble faithfulness

26 Pun fully intended.

in cooperation with His grace, but rather through appetites and forbidden knowledge. It is an outgrowth of the original transgression in Eden, magnified to a planet-wide scale. The devil offered this shortcut to Eve, which was a transgression not only of appetite and forbidden knowledge but was an attempt to become like God but without the obedient relationship with Him: "But the serpent said to the woman, 'You will not surely die. For God knows that when you eat of it your eyes will be opened, and you will be like God, knowing good and evil'" (Gen. 3:4–5).

That phrase *like God* (*elohim*) in Hebrew is a bit ambiguous. It could mean either "like God" or "like gods." It is unambiguous, however, in the Greek Septuagint (*theoi*) and Latin Vulgate (*dii*) translations—"gods"—showing that this was the understanding both of the third-century BC Jews who made the Septuagint and also St. Jerome, who translated the Vulgate in the fourth century AD.

We began this book with a discussion of how the Scriptures use the word *gods,* and so it should be no surprise that Christians would understand *like gods* also to mean "like the angels." This is exactly what one finds, for instance, in the late tenth-century Old English translation of Genesis 3:5, where Ælfric of Eynsham translates *sicut dii* ("like gods") from the Vulgate to *englum gelice* ("like angels").[27]

The promise of theosis that God offers to Christians is the promise He offered to Abraham, that his offspring should be blessed as the stars (Gen. 15:5, 22:17, 26:4). As we saw in chapter 2, the heavenly bodies, but especially the stars, are closely associated with angelic beings. Thus, what the devil offered Eve through a deceptive shortcut, God held out in authentic seriousness to Abraham.

---

27 Ælfric of Eynsham, "Homily on the Beginning of Creation," in *The Homilies of the Anglo-Saxon Church,* vol. 1 (London: Richard and John E. Taylor, 1844), https://www.gutenberg.org/files/38334/38334-h/38334-h.htm.

You Will Be Like Angels

Sometimes when someone dies, especially a small child, people will say that God has now received another angel. When I used to hear that, my inner lover of debunking would grind his teeth and silently growl, "People don't become angels when they die!" As I have delved more deeply into the Scriptures, however, I have learned that this popular image, while literally wrong, isn't entirely wrong. In fact, according to the Scriptures, when righteous people die, they become *like* angels. Perhaps the most direct, obvious statement about Christians becoming like angels is from Christ Himself: "for they cannot die anymore, because they are equal to angels and are sons of God, being sons of the resurrection" (Luke 20:36). We should pay special note to these words from Christ Himself here, where He brings together "sons of the resurrection"—clearly a reference to resurrected humans—with "sons of God" and "equal to the angels."

This language from the Gospel of becoming "equal to the angels" has a precedent in the works of Philo, an Alexandrian Jew born a generation before Jesus. He says of Abraham that he, "leaving mortal things, 'is added to the people of God,' having received immortality, and having become equal to the angels; for the angels are the host of God, being incorporeal and happy souls."[28] So this comparison of immortality as becoming like the angels is found not only in the New Testament but before, paired here explicitly with what God gave to Abraham. One of the most famous New Testament examples is in Acts. Right before St. Stephen is martyred, Acts 6:15 says that his face is "like the face of an angel." His place as the protomartyr must have set up the pattern for interpreting martyrdom in angelic terms, as we soon see in the *Martyrdom of*

28 Philo of Alexandria, "A Treatise on the Sacrifices of Abel and Cain," *Early Christian Writings,* II, http://www.earlychristianwritings.com/yonge/book6.html.

Polycarp that those about to be martyred were "no longer men, but already angels."[29]

Additionally, St. John Cassian connects the phrase "on earth as it is in heaven" from the Lord's Prayer with becoming like angels:

> The third petition is of sons: "Thy will be done on earth as it is in heaven." There cannot be a greater prayer than to desire that earthly things should deserve to equal heavenly ones. For what does it mean to say: "Thy will be done on earth as it is in heaven," if not that human beings should be like angels and that, just as God's will is fulfilled by them in heaven, so also all those who are on earth should do not their own but His will?[30]

Notice also that he says this petition about becoming like angels "is of sons," meaning that humans becoming sons of God imitates what is happening in heaven. Saint John Chrysostom likewise says in several places that the whole purpose of Christ's work was to make humans like angels:

> Great indeed must be the God of the Christians, who makes angels out of men, and renders them superior to all the constraining force of our nature![31]

> For what did not the Cross introduce? The doctrine concerning the Immortality of the Soul; that concerning the Resurrection of the Body; that concerning the contempt of things present; that

29 *Martyrdom of Polycarp* 2.3, in *The Apostolic Fathers Volume II*, trans. Kirsopp Lake (Cambridge, MA: Harvard University Press, 1997), 315.

30 Saint John Cassian, *Conferences*, 342.

31 Saint John Chrysostom, "Homily XXI On the Statues," trans. W. R. W. Stephens, in *Nicene and Post-Nicene Fathers I*, ed. Philip Schaff, vol. 9 (Peabody, MA: Hendrickson Publishers, 1999), 486.

> concerning the desire of things future. Yea, angels it has made of men, and all, everywhere, practice self-denial, and show forth all kinds of fortitude.[32]

> For [Christ] is not at all satisfied with the signs only, but He also threatens hell, and promises a kingdom, and lays down those startling laws, and all things He orders to this end, that He may make us equal to the angels.[33]

There are many other references from patristic literature and liturgical texts we could make here, but suffice it to say that this kind of language is all over Orthodox Tradition.

Angel Language for Humans

In multiple ways, the Scriptures pick up this theme that humans can become like the angels, and perhaps the most obvious is how angel language in the Old Testament gets used to refer to righteous humans in the New Testament. We have discussed in some detail the phrase *sons of God* and shown how it applies in most cases to angels. In addition to Luke 20:36, here are the rest of the references to the phrase in the New Testament:

> But to all who did receive him, who believed in his name, he gave the right to become [sons] of God. (John 1:12)

---

32 Saint John Chrysostom, "Homily IV On First Corinthians," trans. Talbot W. Chambers, in *Nicene and Post-Nicene Fathers I*, ed. Philip Schaff, vol. 12 (Peabody, MA: Hendrickson Publishers, 1999), 19.

33 Saint John Chrysostom, "Homily XLVI On Matthew," trans. George Prevost, in *Nicene and Post-Nicene Fathers I*, ed. Philip Schaff, vol. 12 (Peabody, MA: Hendrickson Publishers, 1999), 291.

> Blessed are the peacemakers, for they shall be called sons of God. (Matt. 5:9)

> For all who are led by the Spirit of God are sons of God. . . . For the creation waits with eager longing for the revealing of the sons of God. (Rom. 8:14, 19)

> For in Christ Jesus you are all sons of God, through faith. (Gal. 3:26)

> See what kind of love the Father has given to us, that we should be called the [sons] of God; and so we are. (1 John 3:1)[34]

There is another word in the Old Testament that generally applies to angels, but the New Testament begins to apply it to humans, and that is *saints,* or *holy ones.* (In the original languages of the Scriptures, there are not two words for this, whether in the noun or adjective form, though in English we have *saint* for the noun and *holy* for the adjective.) God is many times said to come in the company of His "holy ones" or "saints," often numbered in the thousands—this is a reference to God as the Lord of Hosts, who are the angelic armies.[35]

There are too many references in the New Testament to make an appropriate list, but one can see *saint* used there to refer both to living Christians on earth and also to those who have died in the body and are with Christ. The Orthodox Tradition connects this angelic *saint* language to humans not only in terms of the literal sense of holiness but also as a reference to humans being added to the armies of God, which this hymn expresses, for instance:

---

34 Rather than the usual *uioi,* John 1:12 and 1 John 3:1 use *teknon,* which can also be translated "children," which is how the ESV renders it in John 1:12.

35 E.g., Deut. 33:2; Job 5:1, 15:5; Ps. 89:5–7; Dan. 4:17; Jude 14.

> He was willing to appear incarnate from [the Virgin Mary] without father, renewing the creation of His likeness, corrupt with suffering, in order to find the sheep lost in the hills, and carry it on His shoulders, and offer it to the Father, and add it, through His will, to the heavenly hosts, and to save the whole world; for He is the reigning Christ, Possessor of rich and great mercy.[36]

In this hymn, renewing the creation from corruption, finding and saving the lost, bringing them to the Father, adding them to the heavenly hosts, and bringing salvation to the whole cosmos are all bound up in the action of Christ's Incarnation and His kingship amidst the divine council.

Angel Tasks for Humans

One of the things that is most perplexing to Protestant Christians about Orthodox Christianity is the Orthodox approach to saints. The interaction that Orthodox Christians have with saints might feel like worship to Protestants, and saints themselves might feel like an extraneous addition that obscures the Christian Faith. As we've seen, however, the Scriptures take angel language and apply it to righteous humans, especially in the New Testament. We also see that the way angels function in the Scriptures also applies to holy humans. Thus, the way Orthodox Christians treat human saints should already be familiar to anyone who knows the Scriptures and sees how angels are treated. What already applies to angels is being extended to holy humans.

Here is the evidence from Scripture. In the Scriptures, angels do the following:

---

36 Tone 4 Dogmatic Theotokion, Great Vespers.

1. Deliver messages from God (Zech. 1:12–21; Matt. 1:20–21; Luke 1:11–13; Acts 7:53; Heb. 2:2; Rev. 1:4, 14:6)
2. Worship and serve at the throne of God (Neh. 9:6; Rev. 4:6–11, 5:11, 7:11–12)
3. Witness to and receive the calls of the people of God (Gen. 19:20; Job 5:1; Ps. 30:4, 103:20, 148:2; 1 Tim. 5:21)
4. Intercede at the throne of God (Job 33:23, Matt. 18:10)
5. Pass on the prayers of God's people (Rev. 8:3–4)
6. Protect the people of God and battle demons (Dan. 10:13, 12:1; Ps. 34:7, 78:49, 91:11; Heb. 1:14; Jude 1:9; Rev. 12:7)

Here is the same list of tasks, but applied to holy humans, with references from both Scripture and subsequent Church history:

1. Deliver messages from God (Prophets in the Old Testament, Rev. 5:5, all human saints in the New Testament and beyond)
2. Worship and serve at the throne of God (Moses and Elias at Transfiguration, Twenty-Four Elders in Rev. 4, 5, 7, 19)
3. Witness to and receive the calls of the people of God (Luke 15:7, Heb. 12:1, Rev. 18:20)
4. Intercede at the throne of God (2 Macc. 15:14–17; Rev. 1:6, 5:10, 20:6—saints are priests; intercession is part of that)
5. Pass on the prayers of God's people (Rev. 5:8–10)
6. Protect the people of God and battle demons (Dan. 7:21–27, patron saints, seen throughout Church history)

Certainly, one might argue over the interpretation of a particular verse, but the point is that the way Orthodox Christians view human saints is essentially the same way we view the angelic saints: as glorified, righteous humans simply following the same pattern as their angelic precedents.

Angel Thrones for Humans

The language one encounters in the Orthodox Tradition related to the Virgin Mary, the Theotokos ("birth-giver to God"), also shows us how the Church views human saints in relation to angelic saints. Take this frequently heard hymn to the Theotokos, for instance: "More honorable than the cherubim and more glorious beyond compare than the seraphim, who without corruption gave birth to God the Word—thee do we magnify." In it, we are clearly singing that the Theotokos is above the angels. Does that have any basis in the Scriptures? Yes! For one thing, she herself prophesied that "from now on all generations will call [her] blessed" (Luke 1:48). Further, when she says that God "has brought down the mighty from their thrones"—that is, the domineering demons—she also says that He has "exalted those of humble estate" (Luke 1:52). Here she is simply recognizing what the Scriptures speak of elsewhere, not only about herself but about all the human saints. Let's look at a few of those passages.

Saint Paul, when he corrects the Corinthian Christians in 1 Corinthians 6:2–3 for bringing lawsuits against each other in civil courts, says this: "Or do you not know that the saints will judge the world? And if the world is to be judged by you, are you incompetent to try trivial cases? Do you not know that we are to judge angels? How much more, then, matters pertaining to this life!" In other words, why would they go to civil judges when their own vocation is to "judge the world"? That "judging" does not refer narrowly to court cases but rather the general sense of establishing God's justice, which is about making things right and setting things in order. He even says that this means Christians will judge angels, which, again, places humans above the angels.

Saint Paul writes elsewhere concerning the vocation of humanity, the world to come, and the angels:

> For it was not to angels that God subjected the world to come, of which we are speaking. It has been testified somewhere,
>
> "What is man, that you are mindful of him, / or the son of man, that you care for him? / You made him for a little while lower than the angels; / you have crowned him with glory and honor, / putting everything in subjection under his feet." (Heb. 2:5–8)

This passage of course speaks of Christ, but also, in tandem with the 1 Corinthians verse above, it shows the vocation of holy humans—they will rule over the world that is to come. For now they are lower than the angels, but God will give them glory and honor, and exalt them to a place above the angelic hosts. If the angels assist God in governing the world as it now is, then when human saints reign in the age to come, the angels will continue their current work but they will do it at the direction of righteous humanity.

In that same chapter, St. Paul notes, "For surely it is not angels that he helps, but he helps the offspring of Abraham" (Heb. 2:16), which means that the repentance and exaltation God gives to the faithful He does not offer to angels. This destiny is why St. Paul can also speak of the resurrected saints this way: "So is it with the resurrection of the dead. What is sown is perishable; what is raised is imperishable. It is sown in dishonor; it is raised in glory. It is sown in weakness; it is raised in power" (1 Cor. 15:42–43).

All the examples we have seen in this section explain what the Scriptures mean when they show the faithful on thrones next to Christ and reigning with Him:

> Then I saw thrones, and seated on them were those to whom the authority to judge was committed. Also I saw the souls of those who

> had been beheaded for the testimony of Jesus and for the word of God. . . . They came to life and reigned with Christ for a thousand years. (Rev. 20:4)

> And night will be no more. They will need no light of lamp or sun, for the Lord God will be their light, and they will reign forever and ever. (Rev. 22:5)

The glorious vocation of the saints, and especially of the martyrs, is to be seated on thrones next to Jesus Christ, connected with the cherubic throne of fire as the prophet Daniel prophesied (Dan. 7:9). What does this mean? Not that the saints will be merely in lofty places and look and act like kings but rather that they will participate in God's creative ordering of the world, just as the angels do now—but they are destined to do so in an even higher place.

That glorified humans will take their seats on angelic thrones is supported even further by the traditional belief that the fallen angels, having left their places as co-rulers with God in His creation, are replaced by human saints. The number seventy-two (or seventy) is traditionally associated with angelic governors over the nations (the "number of the sons of God" in Deut. 32:8). In Revelation, twenty-four redeemed human elders appear (Rev. 4:4, 8; 5:8; 11:16; 19:4), a number that matches the third of the stars (angels) that fall from heaven (Rev. 12:4). The number seventy-two also appears with the second set of apostles that Christ appoints in the Gospels. The Gospels number them as either seventy or seventy-two, indicating that God is appointing these missionary saints as new patrons and guardians of the nations.

As we saw earlier, the origin of paganism is the worship of fallen angels whom God had set as guardians over the nations; the people worshiped them as gods in their own right. The saints whom God then sets as patrons over the nations literally replace the pagan gods, the fallen angels:

> From the other part of the rational creation—that is, mankind—although it had perished as a whole through sins and punishments, both original and personal, God had determined that a portion of it would be restored and would fill up the loss which that diabolical disaster had caused in the angelic society. For this is the promise to the saints at the resurrection, that they shall be equal to the angels of God.[37]

However, the saints do not replace the fallen angels in the sense of now being worshiped as gods. Rather, they replace the fallen angels in the sense of resuming the God-given ministry those rebellious angels abandoned, making up for the loss in the heavenly hosts.

Theosis Means Becoming Sons of God

Perhaps the most well-known summary in the Orthodox Tradition of what salvation means is this statement from St. Athanasius: "He was made man in order that we might be made gods."[38] It is a shocking thing to hear without any of the background I have just described. Yet people sometimes quote it as a kind of slogan for what *theosis* ("divinization" or "deification") means, but without the context that St. Athanasius himself gives in the whole of his theology.

---

37 Saint Augustine of Hippo, *Enchiridion: On Faith, Hope, and Love*, trans. and ed. Albert Cook Outler (Philadelphia: Westminster Press, 1955), IX.29, https://www.tertullian.org/fathers/augustine_enchiridion_02_trans.htm.

38 Saint Athanasius of Alexandria, *On the Incarnation* 54:3. For what follows, I am indebted to my late friend Fr. Matthew Baker's paper "Deification and Sonship According to St. Athanasius of Alexandria." This and the other translations of Athanasius are from his paper.

We have already seen that becoming sons of God is the destiny for human saints. Scripture refers to our adoption as sons in many places (Rom. 8:15, 23, 9:4; Gal. 4:5; Eph. 1:5) as well as to being born anew, born from above as children of God (Rom. 8:16–17, John 1:12, 1 John 3:1–2). A particularly striking example appears at the beginning of the Gospel of John: "But to all who did receive him, who believed in his name, he gave the right to become children of God, who were born, not of blood nor of the will of the flesh nor of the will of man, but of God" (John 1:12–13).

In another of his works, St. Athanasius directly connects the Incarnation of Christ with the possibility for adoption as sons of God:

> On this account has the Word become flesh, that, since the word is Son, therefore, because of the Son dwelling in us, He may be called our Father also; for "He sent forth," says Scripture, "the Spirit of His Son into our hearts, crying Abba, Father." Therefore the Son in us, calling upon His own Father, causes Him to be named our Father also. (*Against the Arians* IV, 15.22)

So here we get not just the short statement that God became man so that we might become gods, but rather that the Son of God became incarnate as man so that we might be adopted as sons of God:

> Adoption therefore could not be apart from the real Son, who says, "No one knoweth the Father, save the Son, and He to whomsoever the Son will reveal Him." And how can there be deifying apart from the Word and before Him? Yet, He saith to their brethren the Jews, "If He called them gods, unto whom the Word came." And if all that are called sons and gods, whether in earth or in heaven, were adopted and deified through the Word, and the Son Himself is the Word, it is plain through Him are they all. And He Himself before all, or rather He Himself only is very Son. (*Against the Arians* I, 11.39)

Being made gods and being made sons of God are thus the same single act, and all is done by the indwelling of the Holy Spirit:

> While Christ is the true Son, we are made into sons when we receive the Spirit: "For you have not received," it says, "the Spirit of slavery that leads back to fear. But you have received the Spirit of sonship" (Rom. 8:15). But when we are made sons by the Spirit, it is clearly in Christ that we receive the title "children of God": "For to those who did accept him, he gave power to become children of God" (John 1:12). . . . And when the Spirit is given to us (for the Savior said, "Receive the Holy Spirit" [John 20:22]), it is God who is in us. . . . Such being the correlation (*sustoichia*) and the unity of the Holy Trinity, who would dare to separate the Son from the Father, or the Spirit from the Son or from the Father himself? (*To Serapion* I, 19)

What should we take away from this? That the Trinitarian action of receiving the Spirit so that we might become sons of the same Father in Christ the unique Son of God is what it means to become divinized or deified—this is theosis.

Saint Irenaeus also says this same kind of thing in the third century:

> To whom the Word says, mentioning His own gift of grace: "I said, Ye are all the sons of the Highest, and gods; but ye shall die like men." He speaks undoubtedly these words to those who have not received the gift of adoption, but who despise the incarnation of the pure generation of the Word of God, defraud human nature of promotion into God, and prove themselves ungrateful to the Word of God, who became flesh for them. For it was for this end that the Word of God was made man, and He who was the Son of God became the Son of man, that man, having been taken into the Word, and receiving the adoption, might become the son of God. For by no other means could we have attained to incorruptibility and immortality, unless we had

> been united to incorruptibility and immortality. But how could we be joined to incorruptibility and immortality, unless, first, incorruptibility and immortality had become that which we also are, so that the corruptible might be swallowed up by incorruptibility, and the mortal by immortality, that we might receive the adoption of sons?[39]

For St. Irenaeus, then, the judgment of God comes on those who did not receive adoption as sons, even though God had called them to be gods. As for St. Athanasius, Christ's Incarnation here is also directed toward theosis, toward incorruptibility and immortality, and this is so we might be adopted as sons of God.

In Orthodox Christian Tradition, salvation does not mean merely the popular understanding of "going to heaven when you die." Rather, it means to become part of the heavenly hosts, not to become angels by nature but to become angelic by the grace of God—not identical with but equal to the angels. We participate in God's glory like they do and begin to function like they do.

We become adopted sons of God, becoming like God Himself, gradually becoming by God's grace what Christ is by nature. This is what theosis means. The promises God gave to Abraham that his offspring would be like the stars are fulfilled in those who belong to Christ: "And if you are Christ's, then you are Abraham's offspring, heirs according to promise" (Gal. 3:29).

As Christians, we look to Christ as the Lord of Spirits, the one to whom is due all glory, honor, might, authority, and power. Yet this is not a truth we merely look upon, observing as from a distance our God upon His throne. He has invited us to enter into this glory, to take our places among the angels:

---

39 Irenaeus, *Against Heresies* III.19.1, 448.

> But you have come to Mount Zion and to the city of the living God, the heavenly Jerusalem, and to innumerable angels in festal gathering, and to the assembly [or "church"] of the firstborn who are enrolled in heaven, and to God, the judge of all, and to the spirits of the righteous made perfect. (Heb. 12:22–23)

It is an astonishing thought that is almost impossible for our minds to think: that God our Creator, who is upon His throne and rules the whole cosmos, has set up thrones next to His and beckoned us to join Him. We are called to become blessed as the stars, to become saints, to become sons of the resurrection, to become equal to the angels, to become sons of God.

Conclusion

But you, O Lord, *are enthroned forever; / you are remembered throughout all generations. / You will arise and have pity on Zion; / it is the time to favor her; / the appointed time has come. . . . Let this be recorded for a generation to come, / so that a people yet to be created may praise the* Lord: */ that he looked down from his holy height; / from heaven the* Lord *looked at the earth, / to hear the groans of the prisoners, / to set free those who were doomed to die.*

—Psalm 102:12–13, 18–20

For when Satan is bound, man is set free; since "none can enter a strong man's house and spoil his goods, unless he first bind the strong man himself."

—St. Irenaeus of Lyons[1]

1 Irenaeus, *Against Heresies* V.21.3, 550.

THE STORY OF HUMAN REDEMPTION from demons, sin, and death, from all the dark powers of evil, finds its cataclysmic, climactic height in the lowest depths of human experience. There, in Hades itself, the underworld of the dead, our Savior with His lordly might cast down our adversary, the destroyer and accuser, Satan the devil, with utter finality. Christ through His death on the Cross entered the dark underworld and smote the evil one with a blow from which he will never recover, sending the demons fleeing, routed in desperate retreat. He has scattered these proud ones in the imagination of their hearts, casting down the mighty from their thrones (Luke 1:51–52).

The Harrowing of Hades and the Resurrection of Jesus Christ changed everything forever. The decisive battle has been won. The demons are still with us, but they have lost. They and their chief, the devil, are still trying to draw us into damnation with them, but they will never again wield the power they once did. All they have left to them is deception. Against their deceptions we have humility in repentance, and the reason that weapon is so powerful is because by humbling ourselves we join ourselves to Jesus Christ, who in His humility threw down that great dragon and banished him forever at the point of the swords of the archangels, angels, and all the saints.

The great hope of humankind is our Lord Jesus Christ, the Lord of Spirits. In the beginning of human history, because of the envy of the devil, who saw that human destiny was to become adopted sons of God, we were tempted and we fell—into death, into sin, into slavery to demonkind. So began the great war—not a war of human against human but of demons against God, with the weapons of evil turned against humans.

Demons cannot harm the Lord, but they can harm us, who are beloved of the Lord. Spiritual warfare therefore consists of Christ counterattacking His enemies in response to their assault upon us. His victory is sure and He has already won. When we live in accordance with His commandments, we turn away from the works of darkness and communion with demons and toward the works of light and communion with the loving God who made us all.

Every obedience to God is therefore exorcistic. Every time we pray, every time we receive the Holy Mysteries, every time we love, every time we give alms, every time we fast with devotion, every time we feed the hungry, every time we clothe the naked, every time we visit the sick and imprisoned, every time we humble ourselves—with all these faithful actions, we drive out the demons and invite into us the Holy Spirit of God. We become less like the evil ones and more like the Holy One.

The purpose of this book has been to help us recover, in some small way, a more fully Christian framework for understanding the world as it actually is. If we do not act in accordance with that framework, however, even if we should have great knowledge of the unseen world, then we have nothing, or we perhaps have the faith of demons (1 Cor. 13; James 2:14–26). If we love God, however, we keep His commandments (Ex. 20:6; Deut. 5:10, 7:9, 11:1, 11:13; Josh. 22:5; Dan. 9:4; John 14:15, 21, 15:10; 1 John 5:2–3; 2 John 1:6). Understanding this, therefore, we become obedient and faithful to the gospel of Jesus Christ—who He is, what He has accomplished, and what He expects of us.

With the help of the Holy Spirit, especially as expressed through the life of the parish or monastery community, Christians gradually increase their faithfulness, becoming adopted sons of God, equal to the angels, more like Christ. As we do that, we also are able to perceive the world more fully for what it truly is, to understand what the *true* conflicts of our time are about, to interpret what we see through the lenses of Holy Scripture and the whole Orthodox Tradition. Seeing the world as it is, we therefore also become profoundly compassionate toward our fellow humans, who are not our enemies—even if they consciously have decided they are—but are actually afflicted by the demonic powers even as we are. With this compassion, we can then love them as God loves them, taking the initiative to show kindness in imitation of our Savior who died for us even while we were yet sinners (Rom. 5:8).

This, then, is what this title we apply to Jesus Christ means, which is also the title of this book—the Lord of Spirits. And it is why we have this great hope: that in the end, this Son of Man is the Most High God, the Lord of Hosts, the God of gods, the King of kings, the Lord of lords, the Prince over all the angels, the One who presides in the divine council, the Master of all the saints. Christ Jesus, risen from the dead, has trampled down the death god by His death, smashing the gates of Hades. Entering into the darkness of the underworld, He has reached in and pulled out all its captives, bestowing His own glory upon them, for He is the Life.

Aside from the words of Holy Scripture, I have never read anything so moving, so hopeful, or so profound as the account of the Harrowing of Hades in the text The Gospel of Nicodemus. In it is a glorious conclusion to everything that this present book has attempted to convey.

The following is an excerpt from the M. R. James translation of this text, which is also known as The Acts of Pontius Pilate.[2] It is a fourth- or fifth-century compilation of various traditions that dramatizes the events of the Harrowing of Hades, when Christ entered into the underworld through the Cross, defeated the devil, and brought out the righteous into Paradise. As part of the New Testament Apocrypha, it is not canonical Scripture but is nonetheless an edifying text to read outside of church services.[3]

---

2 Montague Rhodes James, trans. and ed., *The Apocryphal New Testament: Being the Apocryphal Gospels, Acts, Epistles and Apocalypses* (Oxford: Clarendon Press, 1924). The original published text is now in the public domain. I have edited it lightly, mainly for formatting and occasionally to update the translation.

3 For analysis of this text, see Fr. Stephen De Young's *Apocrypha*, 233–236.

The text begins with St. Joseph of Arimathea addressing Annas and Caiaphas, two high priests of the Jerusalem temple during the time of Christ, sometime after the Resurrection. It is my personal custom to read this text every year on Holy Saturday, when we celebrate the Harrowing of Hades in the Orthodox Church. I pray that you will read it with hope and with joy.

The Harrowing of Hades

And Joseph arose and said unto Annas and Caiaphas: "Truly and of right do ye marvel because ye have heard that Jesus hath been seen alive after death, and that He hath ascended into heaven. Nevertheless it is more marvelous that He rose not alone from the dead, but did raise up alive many other dead out of their sepulchres, and they have been seen of many in Jerusalem.[4] And now hearken unto me; for we all know the blessed Simeon, the high priest which received the child Jesus in his hands in the temple. And this Simeon had two sons, brothers in blood, and we all were at their falling asleep and at their burial. Go therefore and look upon their sepulchres: for they are open, because they have risen, and behold they are in the city of Arimathea dwelling together in prayer. And indeed men hear them crying out, yet they speak with no man, but are silent as dead men. But come, let us go unto them and with all honour and gentleness bring them unto us, and if we adjure them, perchance they will tell us concerning the mystery of their rising again."

When they heard these things, they all rejoiced. And Annas and Caiaphas, Nicodemus and Joseph and Gamaliel went and found them not in their sepulchre, but they went unto the city of Arimathea, and found them there, kneeling on their knees and giving themselves unto prayer. And they kissed them, and with all

4 Matt. 27:52–53.

reverence and in the fear of God they brought them to Jerusalem into the synagogue. And they shut the doors and took the Law of the Lord and put it into their hands, and adjured them by the Lord and God of Israel who spoke unto our fathers by the prophets, saying: "Believe ye that it is Jesus who raised you from the dead? Tell us how ye have arisen from the dead."

And when Karinus and Leucius heard this adjuration, they trembled in their body and groaned, being troubled in heart. And looking up together unto heaven they made the seal of the cross with their fingers upon their tongues, and forthwith they spoke, both of them, saying: "Give us each a volume of paper, and let us write that which we have seen and heard." And they gave them unto them, and each of them sat down and wrote, saying:

O Lord Jesus Christ, the life and resurrection of the dead, suffer us to speak of the mysteries of Thy majesty which Thou didst perform after Thy death upon the Cross, inasmuch as we have been adjured by Thy Name. For Thou didst command us thy servants to tell no one the secrets of Thy divine majesty which Thou wroughtest in Hades.

Now when we were set together with all our fathers in the deep, in obscurity of darkness, on a sudden there came a golden heat of the sun and a purple and royal light shining upon us. And immediately the father of the whole race of men,[5] together with all the patriarchs and prophets, rejoiced, saying: "This light is the Author of everlasting light who did promise to send unto us His coeternal light." And Isaiah cried out and said: "This is the light of the Father, even the Son of God, according as I prophesied when I lived upon the earth: 'The land of Zabulon and the land of Nephthalim beyond Jordan, of Galilee of the Gentiles, the people that walked in darkness have seen a great light, and they that dwell in the land of the shadow of death,

5 Adam.

upon them did the light shine. And now hath it come and shone upon us that sit in death.'"[6]

And as we all rejoiced in the light which shone upon us, there came unto us our father Simeon, and he rejoicing said unto us: "Glorify ye the Lord Jesus Christ, the Son of God; for I received Him in my hands in the temple when He was born a child, and being moved of the Holy Spirit I made confession and said unto Him: 'Now have mine eyes seen Thy salvation which Thou hast prepared before the face of all people, a light to lighten the Gentiles, and to be the glory of Thy people Israel.'"[7] And when they heard these things, the whole multitude of the saints rejoiced yet more.

And after that there came one as it were a dweller in the wilderness, and he was inquired of by all: "Who art thou?" And he answered them and said: "I am John, the voice and the prophet of the Most High, who came before the face of His advent to prepare His ways, to give knowledge of salvation unto His people, for the remission of their sins. And when I saw Him coming unto me, being moved of the Holy Spirit, I said: 'Behold the Lamb of God, behold Him that taketh away the sins of the world.'[8] And I baptized Him in the river of Jordan, and saw the Holy Spirit descending upon Him in the likeness of a dove, and heard a voice out of heaven saying: 'This is My beloved Son, in whom I am well pleased.'[9] And now have I come before His face, and come down to declare unto you that He is at hand to visit us, even the Dayspring, the Son of God, coming from on high unto us that sit in darkness and in the shadow of death."

And when father Adam that was first created heard this, even that Jesus was baptized in Jordan, he cried out to Seth his son, saying:

6 Is. 9:1–2.
7 Luke 2:25–32.
8 John 1:29.
9 Matt. 3:17; Mark 1:11.

"Declare unto thy sons the patriarchs and the prophets all that thou didst hear from Michael the archangel, when I sent thee unto the gates of paradise that thou mightest entreat God to send thee His angel to give thee the oil of the tree of mercy to anoint my body when I was sick."[10]

Then Seth drew near unto the holy patriarchs and prophets, and said: "When I, Seth, was praying at the gates of paradise, behold Michael the angel of the Lord appeared unto me, saying: 'I am sent unto thee from the Lord: it is I that am set over the body of man. And I say unto thee, Seth, vex not thyself with tears, praying and entreating for the oil of the tree of mercy, that thou mayest anoint thy father Adam for the pain of his body: for thou wilt not be able to receive it save in the last days and times, save when five thousand and five hundred years are accomplished: then shall the most beloved Son of God come upon the earth to raise up the body of Adam and the bodies of the dead, and He shall come and be baptized in Jordan. And when He is come forth of the water of Jordan, then shall He anoint with the oil of mercy all that believe on Him, and that oil of mercy shall be unto all generations of them that shall be born of water and of the Holy Spirit, unto life eternal. Then shall the most beloved Son of God, even Christ Jesus, come down upon the earth and shall bring in our father Adam into paradise unto the tree of mercy.'"

And when they heard all these things of Seth, all the patriarchs and prophets rejoiced with a great rejoicing.

And while all the saints were rejoicing, behold Satan the prince and chief of death said unto Hades: "Make thyself ready to receive Jesus who boasteth Himself that He is the Son of God, whereas He is a man that feareth death, and sayeth: 'My soul is sorrowful even unto

10 This is a reference to traditions found in the Apocalypse of Moses, which includes an account of Adam and Eve's life after the expulsion from Paradise.

death.'[11] And He hath been much mine enemy, doing me great hurt, and many that I had made blind, lame, dumb, leprous, and possessed He hath healed with a word: and some whom I have brought unto thee dead, them hath He taken away from thee."

Hades answered and said unto Satan the prince: "Who is He that is so mighty, if He be a man that feareth death? For all the mighty ones of the earth are held in subjection by my power, even they whom thou hast brought me subdued by thy power. If, then, thou art mighty, what manner of man is this Jesus who, though He fear death, resisteth thy power? If He be so mighty in His manhood, verily I say unto thee He is almighty in His Godhead, and no man can withstand His power. And when He saith that He feareth death, He would ensnare thee, and woe shall be unto thee for everlasting ages."

But Satan the prince of Tartarus said: "Why doubtest thou and fearest to receive this Jesus, who is thine adversary and mine? For I tempted Him, and I have stirred up mine ancient people of the Jews with envy and wrath against Him.[12] I have sharpened a spear to thrust Him through, gall and vinegar have I mingled to give Him to drink, and I have prepared a cross to crucify Him and nails to pierce Him: and His death is nigh at hand, that I may bring Him unto thee to be subject unto thee and me."

Hades answered and said: "Thou hast told me that it is He that hath taken away dead men from me. For there be many which while they lived on the earth have taken dead men from me, yet not by their own power but by prayer to God, and their almighty God hath taken them from me. Who is this Jesus which by His own word without

---

11 Matt. 26:38; Mark 14:34.

12 This line is a recapitulation of what happens in the Gospels, and the Gospels are embedded in the tradition of Israel, which means that this should not be read as anti-Semitic. The Jews of the first century, as part of Israel, are actually God's people, not Satan's. The leaders of first-century Judea, however, were complicit in the events of Christ's death.

prayer hath drawn dead men from me? Perchance it is He who by the word of His command did restore to life Lazarus who was four days dead and stank and was corrupt, whom I held here dead."

Satan the prince of death answered and said: "It is that same Jesus."

When Hades heard that he said unto him: "I adjure thee by thy strength and mine own that thou bring Him not unto me. For at that time I, when I heard the command of His word, did quake and was overwhelmed with fear, and all my ministers with me were troubled. Neither could we keep Lazarus, but he, like an eagle shaking himself, leaped forth with all agility and swiftness, and departed from us, and the earth also which held the dead body of Lazarus straightway gave him up alive. Wherefore now I know that that Man who was able to do these things is a God strong in command and mighty in manhood, and that He is the Saviour of mankind. And if thou bring Him unto me He will set free all that are here shut up in the hard prison and bound in the chains of their sins that cannot be broken, and will bring them unto the life of His Godhead forever."

And as Satan the prince, and Hades, spoke thus together, suddenly there came a voice as of thunder and a spiritual cry: "Lift up your gates, O ye princes, and be ye lifted up, ye everlasting doors, and the King of Glory shall enter in!"[13]

When Hades heard that he said unto Satan the prince: "Depart from me and go out of mine abode: if thou be a mighty man of war, fight thou against the King of Glory. But what hast thou to do with Him?" And Hades cast Satan forth out of his dwelling.

Then said Hades unto his wicked ministers: "Shut ye the hard gates of brass and put on them the bars of iron and withstand stoutly, lest we that hold captivity be taken captive."

13 Ps. 24:7.

But when all the multitude of the saints heard it, they spoke with a voice of rebuking unto Hades: "Open thy gates, that the King of glory may come in."

And David cried out, saying: "Did I not when I was alive upon earth, foretell unto you: 'Let them give thanks unto the Lord, even His mercies and His wonders unto the children of men; who hath broken the gates of brass and smitten the bars of iron in sunder? He hath taken them out of the way of their iniquity.'"[14] And thereafter in like manner Isaiah said: "Did not I when I was alive upon earth foretell unto you: 'The dead shall arise, and they that are in the tombs shall rise again, and they that are in the earth shall rejoice, for the dew which cometh of the Lord is their healing?'[15] And again I said: 'O Death, where is thy sting? O Hades, where is thy victory?'"[16]

When they heard that of Isaiah, all the saints said unto Hades: "Open thy gates: now shalt thou be overcome and weak and without strength."

And there came a great voice as of thunder, saying: "Lift up your gates, O ye princes, and be ye lifted up, ye everlasting doors, and the King of Glory shall enter in!"

And when Hades saw that they so cried out twice, he said, as if he knew it not: "Who is the King of Glory?"[17]

And David answered Hades and said: "The words of this cry do I know, for by His Spirit I prophesied the same; and now I say unto thee that which I said before: 'The Lord strong and mighty, the Lord mighty in war, He is the King of glory.'[18] And: 'The Lord looked down from heaven that He might hear the groanings of them that are in fetters and deliver the children of them that have been slain.'[19]

14 Ps. 107:14–16.
15 Is. 26:19.
16 Hos. 13:14; 1 Cor. 15:55.
17 Ps. 24:8, 10.
18 Ps. 24:8.
19 Ps. 102:19–20.

And now, O thou most foul and stinking Hades, open thy gates, that the King of Glory may come in."

And as David spake thus unto Hades, the Lord of majesty appeared in the form of a man and lightened the eternal darkness and broke the bonds that could not be loosed: and the succor of His everlasting might visited us that sat in the deep darkness of our transgressions and in the shadow of death of our sins.

When Hades and Death and their wicked ministers saw that, they were stricken with fear, they and their cruel officers, at the sight of the brightness of so great light in their own realm, seeing Christ of a sudden in their abode, and they cried out, saying: "We are overcome by Thee! Who art Thou that art sent by the Lord for our confusion? Who art Thou that without all damage of corruption, and with the signs of Thy majesty unblemished, dost in wrath condemn our power? Who art Thou that art so great and so small, both humble and exalted, both soldier and commander, a marvelous warrior in the shape of a bondsman, and a King of Glory dead and living, whom the Cross bare slain upon it? Thou that didst lie dead in the sepulchre hast come down unto us living: and at Thy death all creation quaked and all the stars were shaken: and Thou hast become free among the dead and dost rout our legions. Who art Thou that settest free the prisoners that are held bound by original sin and restorest them into their former liberty? Who art Thou that sheddest Thy divine and bright light upon them that were blinded with the darkness of their sins?"

After the same manner all the legions of devils were stricken with like fear and cried out all together in the terror of their confusion, saying: "Whence art Thou, Jesus, a Man so mighty and bright in majesty, so excellent, without spot and clean from sin? For that world of earth which hath been always subject unto us until now, and did pay tribute to our profit, hath never sent unto us a dead man like Thee, nor ever dispatched such a gift unto Hades. Who then art Thou that so fearlessly enterest our borders, and not only fearest not our torments, but besides essayest to bear away all men out of our bonds? Peradventure Thou art that Jesus, of whom Satan our prince said that by Thy death of the Cross Thou shouldest receive the dominion of the whole world."

Then did the King of Glory in His majesty trample upon Death, and laid hold on Satan the prince and delivered him unto the power of Hades, and drew Adam to Him unto His own brightness.

Then Hades, receiving Satan the prince, with sore reproach said unto him: "O prince of perdition and chief of destruction, Beelzebub, the scorn of the angels and spitting of the righteous, why wouldst thou do this? Thou wouldest crucify the King of Glory, and at His death didst promise us great spoils of His death: like a fool thou knewest not what thou didst. For behold, now, this Jesus putteth to flight by the brightness of His majesty all the darkness of death, and hath broken the strong depths of the prisons, and let out the prisoners, and loosed them that were bound. And all that were sighing in our torments do rejoice against us, and at their prayers our dominions are vanquished and our realms conquered, and now no nation of men feareth us any more. And beside this, the dead which were never wont to be proud triumph over us, and the captives which never could be joyful do threaten us.

"O prince Satan, father of all the wicked and ungodly and renegades, wherefore wouldst thou do this? They that from the beginning until now have despaired of life and salvation—now is none of their wonted roarings heard, neither doth any groan from them sound in our ears, nor is there any sign of tears upon the face of any of them. O prince Satan, holder of the keys of Hades, those thy riches which thou hadst gained by the tree of transgression and the losing of Paradise, thou hast lost by the tree of the Cross, and all thy gladness hath perished. When thou didst hang up Christ Jesus the King of Glory thou wroughtest against thyself and against me. Henceforth thou shalt know what eternal torments and infinite pains thou art to suffer in my keeping forever.

"O prince Satan, author of death and head of all pride, thou oughtest first to have sought out matter of evil in this Jesus: Wherefore didst thou adventure without cause to crucify Him unjustly against whom thou foundest no blame, and to bring into our realm the innocent and righteous One, and to lose the guilty and the ungodly and unrighteous of the whole world?"

And when Hades had spoken thus unto Satan the prince, then said the King of Glory unto Hades: "Satan the prince shall be in thy power unto all ages in the stead of Adam and his children, even those that are My righteous ones."

And the Lord stretching forth His hand, said: "Come unto Me, all ye My saints which bear Mine image and My likeness. Ye that by the tree and the devil and death were condemned, behold now the devil and death condemned by the tree."

And forthwith all the saints were gathered in one under the hand of the Lord. And the Lord holding the right hand of Adam, said unto him: "Peace be unto thee with all thy children that are My righteous ones."

But Adam, casting himself at the knees of the Lord, entreated Him with tears and beseechings, and said with a loud voice: "I will magnify Thee, O Lord, for Thou hast set me up and not made my foes to triumph over me: O Lord my God, I cried unto Thee and Thou hast healed me; Lord, Thou hast brought my soul out of Hades, Thou hast delivered me from them that go down to the pit. Sing praises unto the Lord all ye saints of His, and give thanks unto Him for the remembrance of His holiness. For there is wrath in His indignation and life is in His good pleasure."[20]

---

20 Ps. 30:1–5.

In like manner all the saints of God kneeled and cast themselves at the feet of the Lord, saying with one accord: "Thou art come, O Redeemer of the world: that which Thou didst foretell by the Law and by Thy prophets, that hast Thou accomplished in deed. Thou hast redeemed the living by Thy Cross, and by the death of the Cross Thou hast come down unto us, that Thou mightest save us out of Hades and death through Thy majesty. O Lord, like as Thou hast set the name of Thy glory in the heavens and set up Thy Cross for a token of redemption upon the earth, so, Lord, set Thou up the sign of the victory of Thy Cross in Hades, that death may have no more dominion."

And the Lord stretched forth His hand and made the sign of the cross over Adam and over all His saints, and He took the right hand of Adam and went up out of Hades, and all the saints followed Him.

Then did holy David cry aloud and say: "Sing unto the Lord a new song, for He hath done marvelous things. His right hand hath wrought salvation for Him and His holy arm. The Lord hath made known His saving health, before the face of all nations hath He revealed His righteousness."[21]

And the whole multitude of the saints answered, saying: "Such honour have all His saints.[22] Amen, Alleluia."

And thereafter Habakkuk the prophet cried out and said: "Thou wentest forth for the salvation of Thy people to set free Thy chosen."[23]

And all the saints answered, saying: "Blessed is He that cometh in the name of the Lord. God is the Lord and hath showed us light.[24] Amen, Alleluia!"

Likewise after that the prophet Micah also cried, saying: "What God is like Thee, O Lord, taking away iniquity and removing sins?

21 Ps. 98:1–2.

22 Ps. 149:9.

23 Hab. 3:13.

24 Ps. 118:26–27.

And now Thou withholdest Thy wrath for a testimony that Thou art merciful of free will, and Thou dost turn away and have mercy on us, Thou forgivest all our iniquities and hast sunk all our sins in the depths of the sea, as Thou swarest unto our fathers in the days of old."[25]

And all the saints answered, saying: "This is our God for ever and ever, He shall be our guide, world without end.[26] Amen, Alleluia!"

And so spake all the prophets, making mention of holy words out of their praises, and all the saints followed the Lord, crying, "Amen, Alleluia!"

But the Lord holding the hand of Adam delivered him unto Michael the archangel, and all the saints followed Michael the archangel, and he brought them all into the glory and beauty of Paradise. And there met with them two men, ancients of days, and when they were asked of the saints: "Who are ye that have not yet been dead in Hades with us and are set in Paradise in the body?"

Then one of them answering, said: "I am Enoch who was translated hither by the word of the Lord,[27] and this that is with me is Elias the Tishbite who was taken up in a chariot of fire:[28] and up to this day we have not tasted death, but we are received unto the coming of Antichrist to fight against him with signs and wonders of God, and to be slain of him in Jerusalem, and after three days and a half to be taken up again alive on the clouds."[29]

And as Enoch and Elias spoke thus with the saints, behold there came another man of vile habit, bearing upon his shoulders the sign of the cross; whom when they beheld, all the saints said unto him: "Who art

25 Mic. 7:18–20.
26 Ps. 48:14.
27 Gen. 5:24.
28 2 Kin. 2:11.
29 Rev. 11:1–13.

thou? For thine appearance is as of a robber; and wherefore is it that thou bearest a sign upon thy shoulders?"

And he answered them and said: "Ye have rightly said: for I was a robber, doing all manner of evil upon the earth. And the Jews crucified me with Jesus, and I beheld the wonders in the creation which came to pass through the Cross of Jesus when He was crucified, and I believed that He was the Maker of all creatures and the almighty King, and I besought Him, saying: 'Remember me, Lord, when Thou comest into Thy kingdom.' And forthwith He received my prayer, and said unto me: 'Verily I say unto thee, this day shalt thou be with Me in Paradise':[30] and He gave me the sign of the cross, saying: 'Bear this and go unto Paradise, and if the angel that keepeth Paradise suffer thee not to enter in, show him the sign of the cross; and thou shalt say unto him: "Jesus Christ the Son of God who now is crucified hath sent me."' And when I had so done, I spoke all these things unto the angel that keepeth Paradise; and when he heard this of me, forthwith he opened the door and brought me in and set me at the right hand of Paradise, saying: 'Lo now, tarry a little, and Adam the father of all mankind will enter in with all his children that are holy and righteous, after the triumph and glory of the ascending up of Christ the Lord that is crucified.'"

When they heard all these words of the robber, all the holy patriarchs and prophets said with one voice: "Blessed be the Lord Almighty, the Father of eternal good things, the Father of mercies, Thou that hast given such grace unto Thy sinners and hast brought them again into the beauty of Paradise and into Thy good pastures: for this is the most holy life of the Spirit. Amen, Amen."

These are the divine and holy mysteries which we saw and heard, even I, Karinus, and Leucius: but we were not suffered to relate further

30 Luke 23:42–43.

the rest of the mysteries of God, according as Michael the archangel strictly charged us, saying: "Ye shall go with your brethren unto Jerusalem and remain in prayer, crying out and glorifying the resurrection of the Lord Jesus Christ, Who hath raised you from the dead together with Him: and ye shall not be speaking with any man, but sit as dumb men, until the hour come when the Lord Himself suffereth you to declare the mysteries of His Godhead."

But unto us Michael the archangel gave commandment that we should go over Jordan unto a place rich and fertile, where there are many who rose again together with us for a testimony of the resurrection of Christ the Lord. For three days only were allowed unto us who rose from the dead, to keep the Passover of the Lord in Jerusalem with our kindred that are living for a testimony of the resurrection of Christ the Lord: and we were baptized in the holy river of Jordan and received white robes, every one of us. And after the three days, when we had kept the Passover of the Lord, all they were caught up in the clouds who had risen again with us, and were taken over Jordan and were no more seen of any man. But unto us it was said that we should remain in the city of Arimathea and continue in prayer.

These be all things which the Lord bade us declare unto you: give praise and thanksgiving unto Him, and repent that He may have mercy upon you. Peace be unto you from the same Lord Jesus Christ which is the Saviour of us all. Amen.

And when they had finished writing all things in the several volumes of paper they arose; and Karinus gave that which he had written into the hands of Annas and Caiaphas and Gamaliel; likewise Leucius gave that which he had written into the hands of Nicodemus and Joseph. And suddenly they were transfigured and became white exceedingly and were no more seen. But their writings were found to be the same, neither more nor less by one letter.

And when all the synagogue of the Jews heard all these marvelous sayings of Karinus and Leucius, they said one to another: "Of a truth all these things were wrought by the Lord, and blessed be the Lord, world without end, Amen." And they went out all of them in great trouble of mind, smiting their breasts with fear and trembling, and departed every man unto his own home.

And all these things which were spoken by the Jews in their synagogue, did Joseph and Nicodemus forthwith declare unto the governor. And Pilate himself wrote all the things that were done and said concerning Jesus by the Jews, and laid up all the words in the public books of his judgment hall.

Scripture Index

Old Testament

New Testament

Extracanonical

Subject Index

E

K

L

M

N

Y

Z

About the Author

The Very Rev. Archpriest Andrew Stephen Damick is cohost of *The Lord of Spirits* podcast, Chief Content Officer of Ancient Faith Ministries, and the former pastor (2009–2020) of St. Paul Antiochian Orthodox Church of Emmaus, Pennsylvania. He is author of several books from Ancient Faith Publishing and hosts or cohosts multiple Ancient Faith Radio podcasts. He resides in Emmaus with his wife Kh. Nicole and their children.

We hope you have enjoyed and benefited from this book. Your financial support makes it possible to continue our nonprofit ministry both in print and online. Because the proceeds from our book sales only partially cover the costs of operating **Ancient Faith Publishing** and **Ancient Faith Radio**, we greatly appreciate the generosity of our readers and listeners. Donations are tax deductible and can be made at **www.ancientfaith.com.**

To view our other publications,
please visit our wesite:
store.ancientfaith.com

Bringing you Orthodox Christian music, readings, prayers, teaching, and podcasts 24 hours a day since 2004 at
www.ancientfaith.com